A THEORY OF EVERYTHING

A THEORY OF EVERYTHING

*An Integral Vision
for Business, Politics,
Science, and Spirituality*

Ken Wilber

SHAMBHALA
Boston
2000

SHAMBHALA PUBLICATIONS, INC.
Horticultural Hall
300 Massachusetts Avenue
Boston, Massachusetts 02115
www.shambhala.com

9 8 7 6 5 4 3 2 1

FIRST EDITION
Printed in the United States of America
⊗ This edition is printed on acid-free paper that meets the
American National Standards Institute z39.48 Standard.
Distributed in the United States by Random House, Inc.,
and in Canada by Random House of Canada Ltd

Library of Congress Cataloging-in-Publication Data
Wilber, Ken.
A theory of everything: an integrated vision for business,
politics, science, and spirituality/Ken Wilber — 1st ed.
p. cm.
Includes index.
ISBN 1-57062-724-X
1. Life I. Title
BD431 .W5155 2000
191--dc21
00-040024

Contents

A Note to the Reader

A T THE DAWN OF THE MILLENNIUM, what's the hottest item on the intellectual front? An item that commands the interest of academia as well as intellectual fashion magazines such as *Atlantic Monthly* and the *New Yorker*? That captures public interest as well as professorial? That promises finally to reveal long-hidden secrets of the human condition? Whose terms those "in the know" can quickly name, if not explain, and thus beam with this searingly hot new idea?

Some would say evolutionary psychology, which is the application of evolutionary principles to the study of human behavior: you know, human males are sexually profligate and females are nest-builders because a million years of natural selection have made us so. Evolutionary psychology has indeed become a very hot item, largely because it has managed to displace three decades of postmodernism, which previously was the megahip item but is now met with a slow yawn and casual scorn: postmodernism is *so* yesterday (and isn't that *ironic?*). Postmodernism had built its huge band of followers largely on its capacity to deconstruct everybody else's ideas, leaving the wielder of this postmodernist demolition as the king or queen of the academic hill.

Evolutionary psychology managed to pull the rug out from under the rug-pullers, and it did so by showing that evolutionary principles give much more interesting and compelling explanations of human behavior than the standard postmodern claim that all behavior is culturally relative and socially constructed. Evolutionary psychology made it clear that there are indeed universals in the human condition, that evolution can be denied only by embracing incoherence, and that, most of all, postmodernism just wasn't any fun any more.

Evolutionary psychology is actually a branch of a radically new understanding of evolution itself. The previous neo-Darwinian synthesis saw evolution as the result of random genetic mutations, the more favorable of which (in terms of survival value) are carried forward by natural selection. This theory always left many people with a deeply uncomfortable feeling: how could all of the extraordinary vitality and diversity of life come from a universe that is supposed to be governed solely by the laws of physics, laws that bluntly assert that the universe is running down? The second law of thermodynamics tells us that in the real world, disorder always increases. Yet simple observation tells us that, in the real world, life creates order everywhere: the universe is winding up, not down.

The revolutionary new understanding found in "chaos" and "complexity" theories maintains that the physical universe actually has an inherent tendency to create order, just as when water chaotically washing down the drain in your bathroom sink suddenly organizes itself into a beautiful swirling whirlpool. Biological life itself is a series of swirling whirlpools, creating order out of chaos at every turn, and these new and more highly ordered structures are carried forward by various selection processes operating at all levels, from physical to cultural. In the human domain, this shows up in exactly the behavior studied by the new evolutionary psychology—a very hot topic, understandably!

Still, as hot as evolutionary psychology is, it's not the hottest. Starting seriously in the early 1980s and building to something of a crescendo in the late 1990s, the world of physics began to hum with rumors of *a theory of everything*: a model that would unite all the known laws of the universe into one all-embracing theory that would literally explain everything in existence. The very hand of God could be seen in its formulas, some whispered. The veil had been lifted from the face of the ultimate Mystery, others said. The final Answer was at hand, the hushed consensus hinted.

Known as *string theory* (or more accurately, *M-theory*), it promises to unite all of the known models of physics—covering electromagnetism, nuclear forces, and gravity—into one all-encompassing supermodel. The fundamental units of this supermodel are known as "strings," or one-dimensional vibrating chords, and from the various types of "notes" that these fundamental strings play, one can derive every known particle and force in the cosmos.

M-theory (the "M" is said to stand for everything from Matrix to Membrane to Mystery to Mother, as in the Mother of All Theories) is indeed an exciting and promising model, and should it eventually prove sound—it has yet to have any extensive physical corroboration—it would indeed be one of the most profound scientific discoveries of all time. And that is why, for those in the know, string theory or M-theory is the hottest of the hot intellectual stories, an explosively revolutionary supermodel that pushes even evolutionary psychology into the mundane corner of the merely interesting.

M-theory has certainly got intellectuals thinking; that is, thinking differently. What would it mean if there were a theory that explained *everything*? And just what does "everything" actually mean, anyway? Would this new theory in physics explain, say, the meaning of human poetry? Or how economics works? Or the stages of psychosexual development? Can this new physics explain the currents of ecosystems, or the dynamics of history, or why human wars are so terribly common?

In the interiors of quarks, it is said, there are vibrating strings, and these strings are the fundamental units of everything. Well, if so, it is a strange everything, pale and anemic and alien to the richness of the world that daily presents itself to you and me. Clearly strings are an important *part* of a larger world, fundamental to it, but not that significant, it seems. You and I already know that strings, should they exist, are only a tiny part of the picture, and we know this every time we look around, listen to Bach, make love, are caught transfixed at the sharp crack of thunder, sit rapturous at sunset, contemplate a radiant world that seems made of something so much more than microscopic, one-dimensional, tiny rubber bands. . . .

The Greeks had a beautiful word, *Kosmos*, which means the patterned Whole of all existence, including the physical, emotional, mental, and spiritual realms. Ultimate reality was not merely the cosmos, or the physical dimension, but the Kosmos, or the physical and emotional and mental and spiritual dimensions altogether. Not just matter, lifeless and insentient, but the living Totality of matter, body, mind, soul, and spirit. The Kosmos!—now there is a real theory of everything! But us poor moderns have reduced the Kosmos to the cosmos, we have reduced matter and body and mind and soul and spirit to nothing but matter alone, and in this drab and dreary world of scientific materialism, we are lulled into the notion that a theory uniting the physical dimension is actually a theory of *everything*. . . .

The new physics, it is said, actually shows us the mind of God. Well, perhaps, but only when God is thinking about dirt. So without in any way denying the importance of a unified physics, let us also ask: can we have a theory, not merely of the cosmos, but of the Kosmos? Can there be a genuine Theory of Everything? Does it even make sense to ask this question? And where would we begin?

"An integral vision"—or a genuine Theory of Everything—attempts to include matter, body, mind, soul, and spirit as they appear in self, culture, and nature. A vision that attempts to be comprehensive, balanced, inclusive. A vision that therefore embraces science, art, and morals; that equally includes disciplines from physics to spirituality, biology to aesthetics, sociology to contemplative prayer; that shows up in integral politics, integral medicine, integral business, integral spirituality. . . .

This book is a brief overview of a Theory of Everything. All such attempts, of course, are marked by the many ways in which they fail. The many ways in which they fall short, make unwarranted generalizations, drive specialists insane, and generally fail to achieve their stated aim of holistic embrace. It's not just that the task is beyond any one human mind; it's that the task itself is inherently undoable: knowledge expands faster than ways to categorize it. The holistic quest is an ever-receding dream, a horizon that constantly retreats as we approach it, a pot of gold at the end of a rainbow that we will never reach.

So why even attempt the impossible? Because, I believe, a little bit of wholeness is better than none at all, and an integral vision offers considerably more wholeness than the slice-and-dice alternatives. We can be more whole, or less whole; more fragmented, or less fragmented; more alienated, or less alienated—and an integral vision invites us to be a little more whole, a little less fragmented, in our work, our lives, our destiny.

There are immediate benefits, as you will see in the following pages. The first four chapters introduce a Theory of Everything, and the last three outline its relevance in the "real world," where we will discuss integral politics, integral business, integral education, integral medicine, and integral spirituality—as they are already finding widespread and enthusiastic applications. The last chapter discusses "integral transformative practice," or the ways in which an integral approach to psychological and spiritual transformation can be used in your own case, if you so desire.

(The endnotes are for advanced students or for a second reading. And, in the last chapter, I will give recommended readings for those who would like to further pursue the integral vision and a Theory of Everything.)

This book is a companion to *Boomeritis*, because I believe the world in general, and my generation in particular, is now at something of a branch point: we can continue the road of scientific materialism, fragmented pluralism, and deconstructive postmodernism; or we can indeed choose a more integral, more embracing, more inclusive path to travel. Both *Boomeritis* and *A Theory of Everything* therefore start the same: the first chapter and a half are essentially identical in each book. *Boomeritis* then explores the path we have taken to date—the path of fragmentation and alienation—and *A Theory of Everything* explores the alternative path of holism and integrative embrace. Which path we end up taking depends, of course, on you.

Please use the ideas in the following pages as simple suggestions. See if they make sense to you; see if you can improve them; see in any event if they help you bring forth your own integral ideas and aspirations. I once had a professor who defined a good theory as "one that lasts long enough to get you to a better one." The same is true for a good Theory of Everything. It is not a fixed or final theory, simply one that has served its purpose if it helps you get to a better one. And in the meantime, there is the wonder and the glory of the search itself, drenched in the radiance of being from the start, and always already completed before it even begins.

K. W.
Boulder, Colorado
Spring 2000

A THEORY OF EVERYTHING

1

The Amazing Spiral

WE LIVE IN AN EXTRAORDINARY TIME: all of the world's cultures, past and present, are to some degree available to us, either in historical records or as living entities. In the history of the planet Earth, this has never happened before.

It seems hard to imagine, but for humanity's entire stay on this planet—for some million years up to the present—a person was born into a culture that knew virtually nothing about any other. You were, for example, born a Chinese, raised a Chinese, married a Chinese, and followed a Chinese religion—often living in the same hut for your entire life, on a spot of land that your ancestors settled for centuries. From isolated tribes and bands, to small farming villages, to ancient nations, to conquering feudal empires, to international corporate states, to global village: the extraordinary growth toward an integral village that seems humanity's destiny.

So it is that the leading edge of consciousness evolution stands today on the brink of an integral millennium—or at least the possibility of an integral millennium—where the sum total of extant human knowledge, wisdom, and technology is available to all. And sooner or later we will have, of course, a Theory of Everything to explain it all. . . .

But, as we will see, there are several obstacles to that integral understanding, even in the most developed populations. Moreover, there is the more typical or average mode of consciousness, which is far from integral anything and is in desperate need of its own tending. Both of those pressing issues—the integral vision as it relates to the most developed and the modestly developed populations—are some of the central topics of this book. Even if we have a Theory of Everything that charitably embraces all and unduly marginalizes none, will it really benefit all peoples? And how can we help to ensure that it does?

In short, what is the status of the integral vision in today's world, both in the cultural elite and in the world at large? Let us start with the leading edge, and the many obstacles to an integral vision in our cultural elite.

FRAGMENTATION AT THE LEADING EDGE

Integral: the word means to integrate, to bring together, to join, to link, to embrace. Not in the sense of uniformity, and not in the sense of ironing out all the wonderful differences, colors, zigs and zags of a rainbow-hued humanity, but in the sense of unity-in-diversity, shared commonalities along with our wonderful differences. And not just in humanity, but in the Kosmos at large: finding a more comprehensive view—a Theory of Everything (T.O.E.)—that makes legitimate room for art, morals, science, and religion, and doesn't merely attempt to reduce them all to one's favorite slice of the Kosmic pie.

And, of course, if we succeed in developing a truly holistic or integral view of reality, then we will also develop a new type of critical theory—that is, a theory that is critical of the present state of affairs in light of a more encompassing and desirable state, both in the individual and the culture at large. The integral paradigm will inherently be critical of those approaches that are, by comparison, partial, narrow, shallow, less encompassing, less integrative.

We will be exploring this integral vision, this T.O.E., in the following pages. But it is definitely not a final view or a fixed view or the only view; just a view that attempts to honor and include as much research as possible from the largest number of disciplines in a coherent fashion (which is one definition of an integral or more comprehensive view of the Kosmos).[1]

Yet the very attempt itself does raise the interesting question: can a truly integral vision exist in today's climate of culture wars, identity politics, a million new and conflicting paradigms, deconstructive postmodernism, nihilism, pluralistic relativism, and the politics of self? Can a T.O.E. even be recognized, let alone accepted, in such a cultural state? Aren't the cultural elite themselves in as fragmented and rancorous a state as ever? Perhaps the masses of humanity are bent on tribal warfare and ethnocentric cleansing; but what if the cultural elite itself is likewise so inclined?

We are talking, in other words, about the leading edge of consciousness evolution itself, and whether even the leading edge is truly ready for an integral vision. In the end we will find, I believe, that there is some very good news in all this; but first, a little bit of what I see as the bad news.

BOOMERITIS

The baby boomer generation has, like any generation, its strengths and weaknesses. Its strengths include an extraordinary vitality, creativity, and idealism, plus a willingness to experiment with new ideas beyond traditional values. Some social observers have seen in the boomers an "awakening generation," evidenced by an extraordinary creativity in everything from music to computer technology, political action to lifestyles, ecological sensitivity to civil rights. I believe there is much truth and goodness in those endeavors, to the boomers' considerable credit.

Boomer weaknesses, most critics agree, include an unusual dose of self-absorption and narcissism, so much so that most people, boomers included, simply nod their heads in acknowledgment when the phrase "the Me generation" is mentioned.

Thus, it seems that my generation is an extraordinary mixture of greatness and narcissism, and that strange amalgam has infected almost everything we do. We don't seem content to simply have a fine new idea, we must have the new paradigm that will herald one of the greatest transformations in the history of the world. We don't really want to just recycle bottles and paper; we need to see ourselves dramatically saving the planet and saving Gaia and resurrecting the Goddess that previous generations had brutally repressed but we will finally liberate. We aren't able to tend our garden; we must be transfiguring the face of the planet in the most astonishing global awakening history has ever seen. We seem to need to see ourselves as the vanguard of something unprecedented in all of history: the extraordinary wonder of being us.

Well, it can be pretty funny if you think about it, and I truly don't mean any of this in a harsh way. Each generation has its foibles; this appears to be ours, at least to some degree. But I believe few of my generation escape this narcissistic mood. Many social critics have agreed, and not just in such penetrating works as Lasch's *The Culture of Narcissism*, Restak's *Self Seekers*, Bellah's *Habits of the Heart*, and Stern's *Me: The Narcissistic American*. Surveying the present state of cultural studies even in American universities, Professor Frank Lentricchia, writing in *lingua franca: The Review of Academic Life*, concluded: "It is impossible, this much is clear, to exaggerate the heroic self-inflation of academic literary and cultural criticism."

Well, ouch. But it's true that if you peruse books on cultural studies, alternative spirituality, the new paradigm, and the great transformation that will occur if the world simply listens to the author and his or her revolutionary ideas, sooner or later this "heroic self-inflation" starts to get to you. Curious as to what all the self-inflation might actually mean, I researched and wrote a book about this strange affliction that seems to shadow my generation, this odd mixture of remarkably high cognitive capacity and wonderfully creative intelligence coupled with an unusual dose of emotional narcissism. Of course, as I said, all previous generations had their own imperfections aplenty; I am by no means picking on boomers. It is just that "awakening generations" often have a particularly intense downside, simply because they are so intense in general, and for boomers, it appears to be a bit of self-inflation, a love affair *avec soi* (along the lines of Oscar Levant's quip to Gershwin: "Tell me, George, if you had it to do all over again, would you still fall in love with yourself?")

I called the book *Boomeritis*. It chronicled dozens of areas and disciplines where an important but partial truth was blown all out of proportion by an overestimation of the power and importance of the self.[2] In a moment I will briefly outline its general conclusions, only because, as I said, this relates directly to an integral vision and its reception in today's world. The idea is simple enough: the Culture of Narcissism is antithetical to an integral culture (because narcissistic, isolated selves strenuously resist communion). And thus the point remains: is the world ready for integral anything? If not, what is preventing it?

The Waves of Existence

Developmental psychology is the study of the growth and development of the mind—the study of interior development and consciousness evolution. So let us ask: Can developmental psychology shed any light on this problem?

One of the striking things about the present state of developmental studies is how similar, in broad outline, most of its models are. Indeed, in *Integral Psychology* I assembled the conclusions of over one hundred different researchers, and, as one of them summarized the situation, "The stage sequences [of all of these theorists] can be aligned across a common developmental space. The harmony of alignment shown suggests a possible reconciliation of [these] theories. . . ."[3]

From Clare Graves to Abraham Maslow; from Deirdre Kramer to Jan Sinnott; from Jürgen Habermas to Cheryl Armon; from Kurt Fischer to Jenny Wade; from Robert Kegan to Susanne Cook-Greuter, there emerges a remarkably consistent story of the evolution of consciousness. Of course there are dozens of disagreements and hundreds of conflicting details. But they all tell a generally similar tale of the growth and development of the mind *as a series of unfolding stages or waves.*

Few of these developmental schemes are the rigid, linear, clunk-and-grind models portrayed by their critics. Development is a not a linear ladder but a fluid and flowing affair, with spirals, swirls, streams, and waves—and what appear to be an almost infinite number of multiple modalities. Most of today's sophisticated developmental theories take all of that into account, and—more important—back it with substantial research.

Let me give one of them as an example. The model is called Spiral Dynamics, based on the pioneering work of Clare Graves. Graves proposed a profound and elegant system of human development, which subsequent research has validated and refined, not refuted. "Briefly, what I am proposing is that the psychology of the mature human being is an unfolding, emergent, oscillating spiraling process marked by progressive subordination of older, lower-order behavior systems to newer, higher-order systems as an individual's existential problems change. Each successive stage, wave, or level of existence is a state through which people pass on their way to other states of being. When the human is centralized in one state of existence, he or she has a psychology which is particular to that state. His or her feelings, motivations, ethics and values, biochemistry, degree of neurological activation, learning system, belief systems, conception of mental health, ideas as to what mental illness is and how it should be treated, conceptions of and preferences for management, education, economics, and political theory and practice are all appropriate to that state."[4]

Graves outlined around eight major "levels or waves of human existence," as we will see in a moment. But it should be remembered that virtually all of these stage conceptions—from Abraham Maslow to Jane Loevinger to Robert Kegan to Clare Graves—are based on extensive amounts of research and data. These are not simply conceptual ideas and pet theories, but are grounded at every point in a considerable amount of carefully checked evidence. Many of the stage models, in fact, have been carefully checked in first-, second-, and third-world countries.[5] The same is true with Graves's model; to date, it has been tested in more than fifty thousand people from around the world, and there have been no major exceptions found to the general scheme.[6]

Of course, this does not mean that any of these schemes gives the whole story, or even most of it. They are all simply partial snapshots of the great River of Life, and they are all useful when looking at the River from that particular angle. This does not prevent other pictures from being equally useful, nor does it mean that these pictures cannot be refined with further study. *What it does mean is that any attempt to understand humanity's struggle to reach an integral embrace ought to take these studies into account.*

THE HUMAN CONSCIOUSNESS PROJECT

These studies, in fact, appear to be a crucial part of any genuine Theory of Everything. If we are going to include the physical, biological, psychological, and spiritual dimensions of existence, then this important research offers us a more generous overview of the many possibilities of the psychological dimension.

In a sense, this research is the psychological correlate of the Human Genome Project, which involves the scientific mapping of all of the genes in human DNA. Just so, this overall psychological research—this Human Consciousness Project—is a cross-cultural mapping of all of the states, structures, memes, types, levels, stages, and waves of human consciousness.[7] This overall map, as we will see, then becomes the psychological component of a possible Theory of Everything, where it will be supplemented with findings from the physical, biological, cultural, and spiritual dimensions. And, we will also see, this psychological map will help us to understand some of the many obstacles that make it hard for individuals to appreciate a more integral vision of their own possibilities.

We return, then, to Clare Graves's work, which has been carried forward and refined by Don Beck and Christopher Cowan in an approach they call Spiral Dynamics.[8] Far from being mere armchair analysts, Beck and Cowan were participants in the discussions that led to the end of apartheid in South Africa. The principles of Spiral Dynamics have been fruitfully used to reorganize businesses, revitalize townships, overhaul education systems, and defuse inner-city tensions.

Spiral Dynamics sees human development as proceeding through eight general stages, which are also called *memes* (see fig. 1-1). "Meme" is a word that is used a lot nowadays, with many different and conflicting meanings—and many critics say the word has no meaning at all.[9] But for Spiral Dynamics, a meme is simply *a basic stage of development that can be expressed in any activity* (we will see many examples of this as we proceed). Beck and Cowan affirm that memes (or stages) are not rigid levels but flowing waves, with much overlap and interweaving, resulting in a meshwork or dynamic spiral of consciousness unfolding. As Beck puts it, "The Spiral is messy, not symmetrical, with multiple admixtures rather than pure types. These are mosaics, meshes, and blends."[10]

Beck and Cowan use various names and colors to refer to these different memes or waves of existence. The use of colors almost always puts people off, at first. But Beck and Cowan often work in racially charged areas, and they have found that it helps to take peoples' minds off of skin color and focus on the "color of the meme" instead of the "color of the skin." Moreover, as much research has continued to confirm, *each and every individual has all of these memes potentially available to them.* And therefore the lines of social

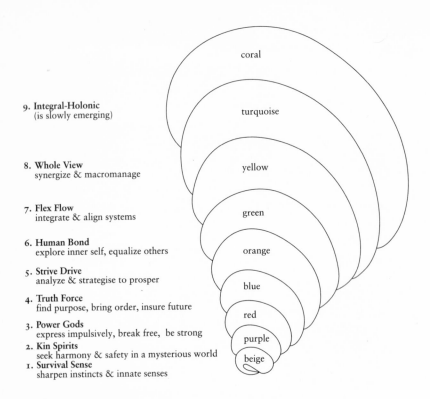

9. Integral-Holonic
(is slowly emerging)

8. Whole View
synergize & macromanage

7. Flex Flow
integrate & align systems

6. Human Bond
explore inner self, equalize others

5. Strive Drive
analyze & strategise to prosper

4. Truth Force
find purpose, bring order, insure future

3. Power Gods
express impulsively, break free, be strong

2. Kin Spirits
seek harmony & safety in a mysterious world

1. Survival Sense
sharpen instincts & innate senses

Figure 1-1. The Spiral of Development. Adapted by permission from Don Beck and Chris Cowan, Spiral Dynamics: Mastering Values, Leadership, and Change *(Cambridge, Mass.: Blackwell Publishers, 1995).*

tension are completely redrawn: not based on skin color, economic class, or political clout, but on the type of meme a person is operating from. In a particular situation it is no longer "black versus white," but perhaps blue versus purple, or orange versus green, and so on; and while skin color cannot be changed, consciousness can. As Beck puts it, "The focus is not on types *of* people, but types *in* people."

The first six levels are "subsistence levels" marked by "first-tier thinking." Then there occurs a revolutionary shift in consciousness: the emergence of "being levels" and "second-tier thinking," of which there are two major waves. Here is a brief description of all eight waves, the percentage of the world population at each wave, and the percentage of social power held by each.[11]

1. *Beige: Archaic-Instinctual.* The level of basic survival; food, water, warmth, sex, and safety have priority. Uses habits and instincts just to survive. Distinct self is barely awakened or sustained. Forms into *survival bands* to perpetuate life.

Where seen: First human societies, newborn infants, senile elderly, late-stage Alzheimer's victims, mentally ill street people, starving masses, shell shock. Approximately 0.1 percent of the adult population, 0 percent power.

2. *Purple: Magical-Animistic.* Thinking is animistic; magical spirits, good and bad, swarm the earth leaving blessings, curses, and spells which determine events. Forms into *ethnic tribes.* The spirits exist in ancestors and bond the tribe. Kinship and lineage establish political links. Sounds "holistic" but is actually atomistic: "There is a name for each bend in the river but no name for the river."

Where seen: Belief in voodoo-like curses, blood oaths, ancient grudges, good-luck charms, family rituals, magical ethnic beliefs and superstitions; strong in third-world settings, gangs, athletic teams, and corporate "tribes." 10 percent of the population, 1 percent of the power.

3. *Red: Power Gods.* First emergence of a self distinct from the tribe; powerful, impulsive, egocentric, heroic. Magical-mythic spirits, dragons, beasts, and powerful people. Archetypal gods and goddesses, powerful beings, forces to be reckoned with, both good and bad. Feudal lords protect underlings in exchange for obedience and labor. The basis of *feudal empires*—power and glory. The world is a jungle full of threats and predators. Conquers, outfoxes, and dominates; enjoys self to the fullest without regret or remorse; be here now.

Where seen: The "terrible twos," rebellious youth, frontier mentalities, feudal kingdoms, epic heroes, James Bond villains, gang leaders, soldiers of fortune, New-Age narcissism, wild rock stars, Attila the Hun, *Lord of the Flies.* 20 percent of the population, 5 percent of the power.

4. *Blue: Mythic Order.* Life has meaning, direction, and purpose, with outcomes determined by an all-powerful Other or Order. This righteous Order enforces a code of conduct based on abso-

lutist and unvarying principles of "right" and "wrong." Violating the code or rules has severe, perhaps everlasting repercussions. Following the code yields rewards for the faithful. Basis of *ancient nations*. Rigid social hierarchies; paternalistic; one right way and only one right way to think about everything. Law and order; impulsivity controlled through guilt; concrete-literal and fundamentalist belief; obedience to the rule of Order; strongly conventional and conformist. Often "religious" or "mythic" [in the mythic-membership sense; Graves and Beck refer to it as the "saintly/absolutistic" level], but can be secular or atheistic Order or Mission.

Where seen: Puritan America, Confucian China, Dickensian England, Singapore discipline, totalitarianism, codes of chivalry and honor, charitable good deeds, religious fundamentalism (e.g., Christian and Islamic), Boy and Girl Scouts, "moral majority," patriotism. 40 percent of the population, 30 percent of the power.

5. *Orange: Scientific Achievement.* At this wave, the self "escapes" from the "herd mentality" of blue, and seeks truth and meaning in individualistic terms—hypothetico-deductive, experimental, objective, mechanistic, operational—"scientific" in the typical sense. The world is a rational and well-oiled machine with natural laws that can be learned, mastered, and manipulated for one's own purposes. Highly achievement oriented, especially (in America) toward materialistic gains. The laws of science rule politics, the economy, and human events. The world is a chessboard on which games are played as winners gain preeminence and perks over losers. Marketplace alliances; manipulate earth's resources for one's strategic gains. Basis of *corporate states*.

Where seen: The Enlightenment, Ayn Rand's *Atlas Shrugged*, Wall Street, emerging middle classes around the world, cosmetics industry, trophy hunting, colonialism, the Cold War, fashion industry, materialism, secular humanism, liberal self-interest. 30 percent of the population, 50 percent of the power.

6. *Green: The Sensitive Self.* Communitarian, human bonding, ecological sensitivity, networking. The human spirit must be freed from greed, dogma, and divisiveness; feelings and caring

supersede cold rationality; cherishing of the earth, Gaia, life. Against hierarchy; establishes lateral bonding and linking. Permeable self, relational self, group intermeshing. Emphasis on dialogue, relationships. Basis of *value communities* (i.e., freely chosen affiliations based on shared sentiments). Reaches decisions through reconciliation and consensus (downside: interminable "processing" and incapacity to reach decisions). Refresh spirituality, bring harmony, enrich human potential. Strongly egalitarian, antihierarchy, pluralistic values, social construction of reality, diversity, multiculturalism, relativistic value systems; this worldview is often called *pluralistic relativism*. Subjective, nonlinear thinking; shows a greater degree of affective warmth, sensitivity, and caring, for earth and all its inhabitants.

Where seen: Deep ecology, postmodernism, Netherlands idealism, Rogerian counseling, Canadian health care, humanistic psychology, liberation theology, cooperative inquiry, World Council of Churches, Greenpeace, animal rights, ecofeminism, post-colonialism, Foucault/Derrida, politically correct, diversity movements, human rights issues, ecopsychology. 10 percent of the population, 15 percent of the power.

With the completion of the green meme, human consciousness is poised for a quantum jump into "second-tier thinking." Clare Graves referred to this as a "momentous leap," where "a chasm of unbelievable depth of meaning is crossed." In essence, with second-tier consciousness, one can think *both* vertically and horizontally, using both hierarchies and heterarchies (both ranking and linking). One can therefore, for the first time, *vividly grasp the entire spectrum of interior development*, and thus see that each level, each meme, each wave is crucially important for the health of the overall Spiral.

As I would word it, each wave is "transcend and include." That is, each wave goes beyond (or transcends) its predecessor, and yet it includes or embraces it in its own makeup. For example, a cell transcends but includes molecules, which transcend but include atoms. To say that a molecule goes beyond an atom is not to say that molecules hate atoms, but that they love them: they embrace them in their own makeup; they include them, they don't marginalize them. Just so, each wave of existence is a fundamental ingredient of all subsequent waves, and thus each is to be cherished and embraced.

Moreover, each wave can itself be activated or reactivated as life circumstances warrant.[12] In emergency situations, we can activate red power drives; in response to chaos, we might need to activate blue order; in looking for a new job, we might need orange achievement drives; in marriage and with friends, close green bonding. All of these memes have something important to contribute.

But what none of the first-tier memes can do, on their own, is fully appreciate the existence of the other memes. Each of the first-tier memes thinks that its worldview is the correct or best perspective. It reacts negatively if challenged; it lashes out, using its own tools, whenever it is threatened. Blue order is very uncomfortable with both red impulsiveness and orange individualism. Orange individualism thinks blue order is for suckers and green egalitarianism is weak and woo-woo. Green egalitarianism cannot easily abide excellence and value rankings, big pictures, hierarchies, or anything that appears authoritarian, and thus green reacts strongly to blue, orange, and anything post-green.

All of that begins to change with second-tier thinking. Because second-tier consciousness is fully aware of the interior stages of development—even if it cannot articulate them in a technical fashion—it steps back and grasps the big picture, and thus second-tier thinking appreciates the *necessary role that all of the various memes play.* Second-tier awareness thinks in terms of the overall spiral of existence, and not merely in the terms of any one level.

Where the green meme begins to grasp the numerous different systems and pluralistic contexts that exist in different cultures (which is why it is indeed the sensitive self, i.e., sensitive to the marginalization of others), second-tier thinking goes one step further. It looks for the rich contexts that link and join these pluralistic systems, and thus it takes these separate systems and begins to embrace, include, and integrate them into holistic spirals and integral meshworks. Second-tier thinking, in other words, is instrumental in moving from relativism to holism, or from *pluralism* to *integralism.*

The extensive research of Graves, Beck, and Cowan indicates that there are at least two major waves to this second-tier integral consciousness:

7. *Yellow: Integrative.* Life is a kaleidoscope of natural hierarchies [holarchies], systems, and forms. Flexibility, spontaneity, and functionality have the highest priority. Differences and plur-

alities can be integrated into interdependent, natural flows. Egalitarianism is complemented with natural degrees of ranking and excellence. Knowledge and competency should supersede power, status, or group sensitivity. The prevailing world order is the result of the existence of different levels of reality (memes) and the inevitable patterns of movement up and down the dynamic spiral. Good governance facilitates the emergence of entities through the levels of increasing complexity (nested hierarchy). 1 percent of the population, 5 percent of the power.

8. *Turquoise: Holistic.* Universal holistic system, holons/waves of integrative energies; unites feeling with knowledge; multiple levels interwoven into one conscious system.[13] Universal order, but in a living, conscious fashion, not based on external rules (blue) or group bonds (green). A "grand unification" [T.O.E.] is possible, in theory and in actuality. Sometimes involves the emergence of a new spirituality as a meshwork of all existence. Turquoise thinking uses the entire Spiral; sees multiple levels of interaction; detects harmonics, the mystical forces, and the pervasive flow-states that permeate any organization. 0.1 percent of the population, 1 percent of the power.

With less than 2 percent of the population at second-tier thinking (and only 0.1 percent at turquoise), second-tier consciousness is relatively rare because it is now the "leading edge" of collective human evolution. As examples, Beck and Cowan mention items that include Teilhard de Chardin's noosphere, the growth of transpersonal psychology, chaos and complexity theories, integral-holistic systems thinking, Gandhi's and Mandela's pluralistic integration, with increases in frequency definitely on the way, and even higher memes still in the offing. . . .

THE JUMP TO SECOND-TIER CONSCIOUSNESS

As Beck and Cowan point out, second-tier thinking has to emerge in the face of much resistance from first-tier thinking. In fact, a version of the postmodern green meme, with its pluralism and relativism, has actively fought the emergence of more integrative and holistic thinking. And yet without second-tier thinking, as Graves, Beck, and

Cowan point out, humanity is destined to remain victims of a global "autoimmune disease," where various memes turn on each other in an attempt to establish supremacy.

This is why many arguments are not really a matter of the better *objective* evidence, but of the *subjective level* of those arguing. No amount of orange scientific evidence will convince blue mythic believers; no amount of green bonding will impress orange aggressiveness; no amount of turquoise holism will dislodge green pluralism—unless the individual is ready to develop forward through the dynamic spiral of consciousness unfolding. This is why "cross-level" debates are rarely resolved, and all parties usually feel unheard and unappreciated.

Likewise, nothing that can be said in this book will convince you that a T.O.E. is possible, unless you already have a touch of turquoise coloring your cognitive palette (and then you will think, on many a page, "I already knew that! I just didn't know how to articulate it").

As we were saying, first-tier memes generally resist the emergence of second-tier memes. Scientific materialism (orange) is aggressively reductionistic toward second-tier constructs, attempting to reduce all interior stages to objective neuronal fireworks. Mythic fundamentalism (blue) is often outraged at what it sees as attempts to unseat its given Order. Egocentrism (red) ignores second tier altogether. Magic (purple) puts a hex on it. Green accuses second-tier consciousness of being authoritarian, rigidly hierarchical, patriarchal, marginalizing, oppressive, racist, and sexist.

Green has been in charge of cultural studies for the past three decades. You will probably already have recognized many of the standard catchwords of the green meme: pluralism, relativism, diversity, multiculturalism, deconstruction, antihierarchy, and so on.

On the one hand, the pluralistic relativism of green has nobly enlarged the canon of cultural studies to include many previously marginalized peoples, ideas, and narratives.[14] It has acted with sensitivity and care in attempting to redress social imbalances and avoid exclusionary practices. It has been responsible for basic initiatives in civil rights and environmental protection. It has developed strong and often convincing critiques of the philosophies, metaphysics, and social practices of the conventional religious (blue) and scientific (orange) memes, with their often exclusionary, patriarchal, sexist, and colonialistic agendas.

On the other hand, as effective as these critiques of pre-green stages have been, green has attempted to turn its guns on all post-green stages as well, with the most unfortunate results. This has made it very difficult, and often impossible, for green to move forward into more holistic, integral constructions.

Because pluralistic relativism (green) moves beyond mythic absolutisms (blue) and formal rationality (orange) into richly textured and individualistic contexts, one of its defining characteristics is its strong *subjectivism*. This means that its sanctions for truth and goodness are established largely by individual preferences (as long as the individual is not harming others). What is true for you is not necessarily true for me; what is right is simply what individuals or cultures happen to agree on at any given moment; there are no universal claims for knowledge or truth; each person is free to find his or her own values, which are not binding on anybody else. "You do your thing, I do mine" is a popular summary of this stance.

This is why the self at this stage is indeed the "sensitive self." Precisely because it is aware of the many different contexts and numerous different types of truth (pluralism), it bends over backwards in an attempt to let each truth have its own say, without marginalizing or belittling any. As with the catchwords "antihierarchy," "pluralism," "relativism," and "egalitarianism," whenever you hear the word "marginalization" and a criticism of it, you are almost always in the presence of a green meme.

This noble intent, of course, has its downside. Meetings that are run on green principles tend to follow a similar course: everybody is allowed to express his or her feelings, which often takes hours; there is an almost interminable processing of opinions, often reaching no decision or course of action, since a specific course of action would likely exclude somebody. Thus there are often calls for an inclusionary, nonmarginalizing, compassionate embrace of all views, but exactly how to do this is rarely spelled out, since in reality not all views are of equal merit. The meeting is considered a success, not if a conclusion is reached, but if everybody has a chance to share their feelings. Since no view is supposed to be inherently better than another, no real course of action can be recommended, other than sharing all views. If any statements are made with certainty, it is how oppressive and nasty all the alternative conceptions are. There was a saying common in the sixties: "Freedom is an endless meeting." Well, the endless part was certainly right.

In academia, this pluralistic relativism is the dominant stance. As Colin McGuinn summarizes it: "According to this conception, human reason is inherently local, culture-relative, rooted in the variable facts of human nature and history, a matter of divergent 'practices' and 'forms of life' and 'frames of reference' and 'conceptual schemes.' There are no norms of reasoning that transcend what is accepted by a society or an epoch, no objective justifications for belief that everyone must respect on pain of cognitive malfunction. To be valid is to be taken to be valid, and different people can have legitimately different patterns of taking. In the end, the only justifications for belief have the form 'justified for me.'"[15] As Clare Graves put it, "This system sees the world relativistically. Thinking shows an almost radical, almost compulsive emphasis on seeing everything from a relativistic, subjective frame of reference."

The point is perhaps obvious: because pluralistic relativism has such an intensely subjectivistic stance, it is especially prey to narcissism. And exactly that is the crux of the problem: *pluralism becomes a supermagnet for narcissism*. Pluralism becomes an unwitting home for the Culture of Narcissism, and narcissism is the great destroyer of any integral culture in general and a T.O.E. in particular (because narcissism refuses to step outside of its own subjective orbit and hence it cannot allow truths other than its own). Thus, on our list of obstacles to a genuine Theory of Everything, we might list the Culture of Narcissism.

And this is where boomeritis enters the picture.

2

Boomeritis

Bore: a person of low taste, more interested in himself
than in me.

—AMBROSE BIERCE

THE DICTIONARY DEFINITION of *narcissism* is "excessive interest in one's own self, importance, abilities, etc.; egocentrism."
Yet narcissism is not simply the overvaluing of the self and its abilities, but a concomitant undervaluing of others and their contributions. It is not simply possessing a large amount of self-esteem; it is
the simultaneous devaluation of others that is crucial. The inner state
of narcissism, clinicians tell us, is often that of an empty or fragmented self, attempting to fill the void with an egocentric grasping
that inflates the self while deflating others. The emotional mood is,
"Nobody tells me what to do!"

Most psychologists agree that, although there are many ways to
look at narcissism (and many different types of narcissism), it is, in
general, a normal trait of childhood that is ideally outgrown, at
least to a significant degree. Development, in fact, can be defined as
a *successive decrease in egocentrism.* The young infant is largely
wrapped up in its own world, oblivious to much of its surroundings
and most human interactions.[1] As its consciousness increasingly
grows in strength and capacity, it can become aware of itself, and of
others, and eventually put itself in others' shoes and thus develop
care, compassion, and a generous integral embrace—none of which
it is born with.

Development as Declining Egocentrism

As Harvard developmental psychologist Howard Gardner reminds us,

> The young child is totally egocentric—meaning not that he thinks selfishly only about himself, but to the contrary, that he is incapable of thinking about himself. The egocentric child is unable to differentiate himself from the rest of the world; he has not separated himself out from others or from objects. Thus he feels that others share his pain or his pleasure, that his mumblings will inevitably be understood, that his perspective is shared by all persons, that even animals and plants partake of his consciousness. In playing hide-and-seek he will "hide" in broad view of other persons, because his egocentrism prevents him from recognizing that others are aware of his location. The whole course of human development can be viewed as a continuing decline in egocentrism.[2]

Thus development, for the most part, involves *decreasing* narcissism and *increasing* consciousness, or the ability to take other people, places, and things into account and thus increasingly extend care to each. Carol Gilligan found, for example, that female moral development tends to go through three general stages, which she calls *selfish, care,* and *universal care*. In each of these stages, the circle of care and compassion expands and egocentrism declines. At first, the young girl cares mostly for herself; then she can care for others as well (such as her family and friends); and finally, she can extend her concern and well wishes to humanity as a whole (and thus move toward an integral embrace). Each higher stage does not mean that you stop caring for yourself, only that you include more and more others for whom you also evidence a genuine concern and compassion.

Incidentally, males go through the same three general stages, although, according to Gilligan, they usually emphasize rights and justice more than care and relationship. Gilligan believes that after the third stage, in both sexes, there can be an *integration* of the contrasexual attitude, so that at the universal-integral stage, both men and women integrate the male and female voices in themselves to a large degree, thus uniting justice and compassion. This integral embrace is a type of culmination of the third general stage of universal care (I will correlate this with other conceptions, such as Spiral Dynamics, in a moment).

Those three general stages are quite common for most forms of development. They are known by many names, such as preconventional, conventional, and postconventional; or egocentric, sociocentric, and worldcentric; or "me," "us" and "all of us."

The selfish stage is often called *preconventional*, because the infant and young child have not yet learned conventional rules and roles; they have not yet been socialized. They cannot yet take the role of others and thus begin to develop genuine care and compassion. They therefore remain egocentric, selfish, narcissistic, and so on. This does *not* mean that young children have no feelings for others, nor does it mean they are altogether amoral. It simply means that, *compared with subsequent development*, their feelings and morals are still heavily centered on their own impulses, physiological needs, and instinctual discharges. (Although some Romantic theorists believe that the infant exists in a state of nondual freedom and original goodness, what baby is truly free? At most, it appears that the infantile state is one of potentiality and openness, not an actual presence of freedom, since any state dominated by impulses, hunger, tension, and discharge cannot be truly free. In any event, studies consistently show that the infant cannot take the role of other, and thus it is not capable of genuine compassion, care, or love.)[3]

Starting around age 6 or 7, a profound shift in consciousness occurs. The child can begin to take the role of other. For example: say you have a book whose front cover is blue and whose back cover is orange. Show the book, front and back, to a five-year-old child. Then hold the book between you and the child. You are looking at the orange cover and the child is looking at blue. Ask the child what color he is seeing, and he will correctly say blue. Ask the child what color *you* are seeing, and he will say blue. A seven-year-old will say orange.

In other words, the five-year-old cannot put himself in your shoes and take your point of view. He does not have the cognitive capacity to step out of his own skin and inhabit yours for a while. And therefore he will never really understand your perspective, will never really understand you; there will never be a *mutual* recognition. Nor can he therefore truly, genuinely, care for your point of view (however much he may emotionally love you). But all of that begins to change with the emergence of the capacity to take the role of others, which is why Gilligan calls this stage the shift from *selfish* to *care*.

The care stage, which generally lasts from age 7 to adolescence, is known as *conventional, conformist, ethnocentric,* or *sociocentric*—and it means just that, centered on the group (family, peers, tribe, nation). The young child steps out of his or her own limited perspective and begins to share the views and perspectives of others—so much so, that the child is often *trapped* in the views of others: hence, conformist. This stage is often called "good boy, nice girl," "my country right or wrong," and so on, reflecting the intense conformity, peer pressure, and group dominance that usually accompanies this general period. Although the individual at this stage can to some degree step aside from her own perspective, she cannot easily step aside from the group's. She has moved from "me" to "us"—a great decline in egocentrism—but there she is stuck, "my country right or wrong."

All of which begins to change in adolescence, with the emergence of *postconventional* and *worldcentric* awareness (Gilligan's *universal* care). This is yet another major decline in egocentrism, because this time one's peer group is subjected to scrutiny. What is right and fair, not just for me or my tribe or my nation, but for all peoples, regardless of race, religion, sex, or creed? The adolescent can become a fiery idealist, ablaze with all the possibilities, a crusader for justice, a revolutionary out to rock the world. Of course, some of this is just an explosion of hormones, frenzied at best. But a good part of it is the emergence of the stage of universal care, justice, and fairness. And, in fact, this is simply the beginning of the possibility of developing a truly integral embrace.

THE SPIRAL OF COMPASSION

These three general stages—egocentric to ethnocentric to worldcentric—are of course just a simple summary of the many unfolding waves of consciousness, but already you can start to see that development, as Gardner said, is indeed a decline in egocentrism. Each developmental wave is a *decrease* in narcissism and an *increase* in consciousness (or an increase in the capacity to take deeper and wider perspectives into account).

There are, of course, more complex models with more stages. In chapter 1 we gave an example of this developmental unfolding using

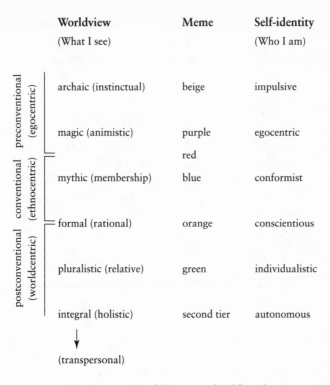

		Worldview (What I see)	Meme	Self-identity (Who I am)
preconventional (egocentric)		archaic (instinctual)	beige	impulsive
		magic (animistic)	purple	egocentric
			red	
conventional (ethnocentric)		mythic (membership)	blue	conformist
		formal (rational)	orange	conscientious
postconventional (worldcentric)		pluralistic (relative)	green	individualistic
		integral (holistic)	second tier	autonomous
		↓		
		(transpersonal)		

Figure 2-1. Worldviews and Selfhood

Spiral Dynamics and its eight waves of development. (See fig. 2-1 for the following correlations.) In Spiral Dynamics, the preconventional stages are beige (archaic-instinctual), purple (magical-animistic), and red (egocentric). Although red is called "egocentric," the first two stages are even more egocentric (there is a steady decline in narcissism at each and every stage); it is just that red marks the culmination of the highly egocentric and preconventional realms and is now able to act this out forcefully. At the next stage (blue, conformist rule), the narcissism is dispersed into the *group*—not me, but my country, can do no wrong! This conventional/conformist stance lasts into orange (egoic-rational), which marks the beginning of the postconventional stages (green, yellow, and turquoise). These postconventional stages (especially orange and green) are marked by an intense scrutiny of the myths, conformist values, and ethnocentric biases that almost always inhabit the preconventional and conventional stages.

In short, as development moves from preconventional to conventional to postconventional (or from egocentric to ethnocentric to worldcentric), the amount of narcissism and egocentrism slowly but surely decreases. Instead of treating the world (and others) as an extension of the self, the mature adult of postconventional awareness meets the world on its own terms, as an individuated self in a community of other individuated selves operating by mutual recognition and respect. The spiral of development is a spiral of compassion, expanding from me, to us, to all of us: there standing open to an integral embrace.

I hasten to add that this does not mean that development is nothing but sweetness and light, a series of wonderful promotions on a linear ladder of progress. For each stage of development brings not only new capacities but the possibility of new disasters; not just novel potentials but novel pathologies; new strengths, new diseases. In evolution at large, new emergent systems always face new problems: dogs get cancer, atoms don't. Annoyingly, there is a price to be paid for each increase in consciousness, and this "dialectic of progress" (good news, bad news) needs always to be remembered. Still, the point for now is that each unfolding wave of consciousness brings at least the possibility for a greater expanse of care, compassion, justice, and mercy, on the way to an integral embrace.

Fight the System!

One source of narcissism, then, is simply the failure to grow and evolve. Particularly in the difficult growth from egocentric to sociocentric, aspects of awareness that refuse this transition can remain "stuck" in the egocentric realms, with a difficulty adapting to the *rules* and *roles* of society. Of course, some of those rules and roles might be unworthy of respect; they might be in dire need of criticism and rejection. But that *postconventional* attitude—which inspects, reflects on, and criticizes the norms of society—can only be attained by first passing through the conventional stages, because the competences gained at those stages are necessary prerequisites for postconventional consciousness. In other words, somebody who fails to make it up to the conventional stages will mount, not a postconventional critique of society, but a preconventional rebellion. The core of narcissism that "Nobody tells me what to do!" is heavily present in the preconventional waves.

The boomers, critics agree, have been a notoriously rebellious generation. Some of that rebellion, no doubt, has come from postconventional individuals sincerely interested in reforming those aspects of society that are unfair, unjust, or immoral. But just as surely—and we have much empirical evidence for this—an alarmingly large chunk of that rebellious attitude has come from preconventional impulses that are having a great deal of difficulty making it up to conventional realities. The standard shouts of the sixties—from "Fight the system!" to "Question all authority!"—can come from preconventional just as easily as from postconventional; and evidence suggests that it was the former more often than the latter.

The classic case study is the Berkeley student protests of the late sixties (protesting especially the Vietnam war). The students claimed, in one voice, that they were acting from a position of higher morals. But when given actual tests of moral development, the vast majority scored at *preconventional*, not postconventional, levels.[4] (There were few conventional/conformist types, because, by definition, they are not very rebellious.) Of course, the postconventional and worldcentric morality of the minority of protestors is to be applauded (not necessarily their beliefs, but the fact that they arrived at them through highly developed moral reasoning). But just as surely, the preconventional egocentrism of the majority of protesters must likewise be acknowledged.

The most fascinating item about such empirical studies is something that is often seen with "pre" and "post" situations—namely, both pre-X and post-X are non-X (for example, both preconventional and postconventional are nonconventional, or outside the conventional norms and rules), and thus they are often confused. In such situations, "pre" and "post" will often use the *same rhetoric and the same ideology*, but in fact they are actually separated by an enormous gulf of growth and development. In the Berkeley protests, virtually all of the students *claimed* they were acting from universal moral principles (e.g., "The war in Vietnam violates universal human rights, and therefore, as a moral being, I refuse to fight in that war"). But tests showed unequivocally that only a minority were acting from postconventional moral principles; the majority were acting from preconventional egocentric drives: "*Nobody tells me what to do! So take your war and shove it.*"

It appears that in this case very high-minded moral ideals were used to support what were in fact much lower-minded impulses. It is the strange superficial similarity of "pre" and "post" stages of development that would allow this subterfuge—that would allow, in other words, preconventional narcissism to inhabit the halls of what was loudly claimed to be postconventional idealism. This confusion of preconventional and postconventional, because both are nonconventional, is called the "pre/post fallacy," and it appears that at least some of boomer idealism must be interpreted, or reinterpreted, in this harsher light.

This is a crucial point, because it alerts us to the fact that, no matter how high-minded, idealistic, or altruistic a cause might appear—from ecology to cultural diversity to world peace—the simple mouthing of intense support for that cause is not enough to determine why, in fact, that cause is being embraced. Too many social commentators have simply assumed, for example, that if the boomers were calling for "harmony, love, mutual respect, and multiculturalism," the boomers were themselves moving in that idealistic, nonegocentric direction. However, as we will see, in many cases not only were the boomers not moving in that direction in terms of their own inner growth, they were loudly embracing a nonegocentric perspective largely to conceal their own egocentric stance.

None of which is to say that all boomers were caught in such. Only that there has often been a strange mixture of postconventional ideas inhabited by preconventional motives, a strange mixture we are calling "boomeritis."

GROWTH HIERARCHIES VERSUS DOMINATOR HIERARCHIES

Pluralism, egalitarianism, and multiculturalism, at their best, all stem from a very high developmental stance—the green meme—and from that stance of pluralistic fairness and concern, the green meme attempts to treat all other memes with equal care and compassion, a truly noble intent.[5] But because it embraces an intense egalitarianism, it fails to see that *its own stance*—which is the first stance that is even capable of egalitarianism—is a fairly rare, elite stance (somewhere around 10 percent of the world's population, as we saw). Worse, the green meme then *aggressively denies* the stages that *produced* the green meme in the first place, because it wishes to view all memes equally and not make any ranking judgments. But green egalitarianism is the product, we have seen, of at least six major stages of development, stages that it then turns around and aggressively denies in the name of egalitarianism!

Much of this pluralistic confusion stems from a misunderstanding of *hierarchy* and its place in natural growth and development. Notice how each of the memes views the notion of hierarchy. Purple (magic) recognizes few hierarchies, largely because, as we will see, it is preformal and preconventional. Red (egocentric power) recognizes hierarchies of brute force (the basis of feudal empires). Blue (mythic order) has numerous and very rigid social hierarchies, such as the hereditary caste system, the hierarchies of the medieval Church, and the intense social stratification of feudal empires and early nations. Orange (individual achievement) decisively erodes blue hierarchies in the name of individual freedom and equal opportunity (orange hierarchies are quite distinct from blue hierarchies in that heredity and privilege yield to meritocracy and excellence).

By the time we get to green, however, the sensitive self begins a concerted attack on, and condemnation of, virtually all types of hierarchies, simply because they have indeed often been involved in horrible social oppression. An aggressive antihierarchy stance is usually an unmistakable hallmark of the green meme.

But with the emergence of second tier, *hierarchies again return*, this time in a softer, nested fashion. These nested hierarchies are often called *growth hierarchies*, such as the hierarchy atoms to molecules to cells to organisms to ecosystems to biosphere to universe.[6] Each of those units, no matter how "lowly," is *absolutely crucial* for the entire sequence: destroy all atoms and you simultaneously destroy all molecules, cells, ecosystems, and so on. At the same time, each senior wave enfolds or envelopes its predecessors—ecosystems contain organisms which contain cells which contain molecules—a development that is envelopment. And thus each wave becomes more inclusive, more embracing, more integral—and less marginalizing, less exclusionary, less oppressive. (Each successive wave "transcends and includes"—transcends its own narrowness to include others.) The developmental Spiral itself is a nested hierarchy or growth hierarchy, as are most natural growth processes. And, indeed, Beck and Cowan point out that nested hierarchies are a hallmark of second-tier thinking.

Riane Eisler, author of *The Chalice and the Blade*, calls attention to this important distinction by referring to "dominator hierarchies"

and "actualization hierarchies." The former are the rigid social hierarchies that are instruments of oppression, and the latter are the
growth hierarchies that are actually necessary for the self-actualiza-
tion of individuals and cultures (and virtually all biological systems
as well). Whereas dominator hierarchies are the means of oppression, actualization hierarchies are the means of growth. It is the
growth hierarchies that bring together previously isolated and fragmented elements. Isolated atoms are brought together into molecules; isolated molecules are brought together into cells; isolated cells
into organisms; organisms into ecosystems; ecosystems into biosphere, and so on. In short, growth hierarchies convert heaps into
wholes, fragments into integration, alienation into cooperation.

And, Spiral Dynamics adds, *all of this becomes increasingly conscious at second tier.* Second-tier integral awareness understands the
nested hierarchy of growth. Thus, if we react negatively to *all* hierarchies, not only will we honorably fight the injustices of dominator
hierarchies, we will very probably prevent ourselves from developing
to the integral second tier. As we will see, the green meme, effectively challenging the absolutisms, universals, and dominator hierarchies
of blue and orange, then mistook all hierarchies as being of the same
order, and because it then denied all hierarchies, this firmly locked it
into first-tier thinking.

(The same thing happens with both "universals" and "metanarratives." They are absent in the preconventional waves; exist in rigid
and oppressive ways at blue; are attacked and deconstructed at
green; then return in a softer, nested fashion at all second-tier integral waves. Whenever you hear an attack on metanarratives and universals, you are almost always in the presence of a green meme.)

BOOMERITIS

The point is simply that the very high developmental stance of green
pluralism—the product of at least six major stages of hierarchical
transformation—turns around and denies all hierarchies, *denies the
very path that produced its own noble stance.* It consequently
extends an egalitarian embrace to every stance, no matter how shallow or narcissistic. The more egalitarianism is implemented, the
more it invites, indeed encourages, the Culture of Narcissism. And
the Culture of Narcissism is the antithesis of the integral culture.

(We saw that narcissism, at its core, is a demand that "Nobody tells me what to do!" Narcissism will therefore not acknowledge anything universal, because that places various demands and duties on narcissism that it will strenuously try to deconstruct, because "nobody tells me what to do." This egocentric stance can easily be propped up and supported with the tenets of pluralistic relativism.)

In short, the rather high developmental wave of pluralism becomes a supermagnet for the rather low state of emotional narcissism. Which brings us to boomeritis.

Boomeritis is that strange mixture of very high cognitive capacity (the green meme and noble pluralism) infected with rather low emotional narcissism—exactly the mixture that has been noted by so many social critics. In other words, the very high developmental meme of pluralism becomes a shelter and a haven for a *reactivation* of some of the lower and intensely egocentric memes (e.g., purple and red). In green's noble attempt to move beyond conformist rules (many of which are indeed unfair and marginalizing), and in its genuine desire to deconstruct a rigid rationality (much of which can be repressive and stultifying)—in short, in green's admirable attempt to go *postconventional*—it has often inadvertently embraced anything nonconventional, and this includes much that is frankly *preconventional*, regressive, and narcissistic.

This strange mixture of very high postconventional memes with preconventional narcissistic memes is boomeritis. A typical result is that the sensitive self, honestly trying to help, excitedly exaggerates its own significance. It will possess the new paradigm, which heralds the greatest transformation in the history of the world; it will completely revolutionize society as we know it; it will revision everything that came before it; it will save the planet and save Gaia and save the Goddess; it will be the most extraordinary. . . .

Well, and off we go on some of the negative aspects of the last three decades of boomer cultural studies. This is exactly why observers on the scene have reported, as we saw with Lentricchia, that "it is impossible, this much is clear, to exaggerate the heroic self-inflation of academic literary and cultural criticism." Once again, that is not the whole story, or even the most important part of the story, of the boomers. But it appears to be an unmistakable flavor. Boomeritis has significantly tilted and prejudiced academic studies; it is behind much of the culture wars; it haunts almost every corner of the New Age; it drives many of the games of deconstruction and identity politics; it authors new paradigms daily. Virtually no topic, no matter how innocent, has escaped a reworking at its hands, as I attempt to document at length in *Boomeritis.*

Since, in normal development, green pluralism eventually gives way to second-tier consciousness and an integral embrace, why did this generation become so stuck at the green meme?—at pluralistic relativism, extreme egalitarianism, antihierarchy furies, deconstructive postmodernism, fragmenting pluralism, I do my thing and you do yours and to hell with integral anything? One of the central reasons appears to be that the intense subjectivism of the green meme was a prime magnet and refuge for the narcissism that, for whatever reasons, many social critics have found prevalent in the Me generation. It appears that boomeritis intensifies a *fixation* to the green meme, making it almost impossible to let go of. Because narcissism finds such a happy home in pluralism, both get stuck with each other. This combination of high pluralism and low narcissism is boomeritis, and it follows that boomeritis is one of the primary roadblocks to an integral embrace.

THE MANY GIFTS OF GREEN

Boomeritis is still one of the single greatest barriers to an integral unfolding, I believe. But the truly important point is not what has gone wrong with green, but what can go right. *For it is from the large fund of green memes that the second tier emerges.*[7] It is from the pluralistic perspectives freed by green that integrative and holistic networks are built.

That fact is worth emphasizing. Development tends to proceed by differentiation and integration (e.g., a single-cell zygote *differentiates* into two cells, then four cells, then sixteen, then thirty-two . . . , while at the same time these differentiated cells are *integrated* into coherent tissues, organs, and systems). The green meme heroically manages to differentiate the often rigid, abstract, universal formalism of the previous rational wave (formal operational, egoic-rational, orange meme). Green therefore discloses, not a rational uniformitarianism that tends to ignore and marginalize anything not of its ilk, but a beautiful tapestry of multiple contexts, richly different cultural textures, pluralistic perceptions, and individual differences, and it becomes sensitive (the sensitive self!) to all of those often unheard voices. We have seen that every meme makes an invaluable contribution to the health of the overall spiral, and this pluralistic sensitivity is the one of the great gifts of green.

Once those wonderful differentiations are made, they can then be brought together into even deeper and wider contexts that disclose a truly holistic and integral world: the leap to second-tier consciousness can occur—but only because of the work that the green meme has accomplished. There is first differentiation, then integration. Second tier completes the task begun by green, and this allows us to move from pluralistic relativism to universal integralism (e.g., mature vision-logic, Gebser's integral-aperspectival, Loevinger's integrated stage, etc.). That is what I mean when I say that the green meme frees the pluralistic perspectives that second tier will integrate.

In short, since green is the conclusion of first-tier thinking, it prepares the leap to second tier. But in order to move into second-tier constructions, the fixation to pluralistic relativism and the green meme in general needs to be relaxed. Its accomplishments will be fully included and carried forward. But its attachment to its own stance needs to be eased, and it is precisely boomeritis (or a narcissistic attachment to the intense subjectivism of the relativistic stance) that makes such a letting-go quite difficult. By highlighting our fixation to the green meme, I believe that we can begin more readily to transcend and include its wonderful accomplishments in an even more generous embrace.

BEYOND PLURALISM

But why is boomeritis one of greatest obstacles to the emergence of an integral vision? What about the rigid conformity of mythic-membership (blue)? What about the often nasty materialism of egoic-rationality (orange)? What about the horrible economic conditions of many third-world countries? What about. . . .

Yes, all of that is true. But, as we were saying, it is only *from* the stage of pluralism (green) that integralism can emerge (holistic second tier). Of course, *all* of the pre-green memes also "prevent" the emergence of an integral view. My point—and the only reason I am "picking on" boomers—is that this generation (and Graves's research confirmed this) is the first to significantly evolve to the green wave in large numbers, and thus this is the first major generation that has a real chance to significantly move forward into a mature second-tier consciousness—and to use that consciousness to organize social institutions in a truly integral fashion.

But it has not yet done so to full effect, because it has not yet gone post-green to any significant degree (as we saw, less than 2 percent are post-green). *But it still might do so*; and since it is only from green that it can do so, the boomers are still poised for a possible leap into the hyperspace of second-tier consciousness. That would indeed be a great and historic transformation, one that would have a profound effect on society as we know it. And that is not a grandiose boomeritis claim; it is backed by substantial evidence, particularly from social and psychological developmental studies.

THE INTEGRAL CULTURE

Sociologist Paul Ray has recently found that a new cultural segment, whose members he calls "the cultural creatives," now make up an astonishing 24 percent of the adult American population (or around 44 million people). In order to distinguish them from the previous cultural movements of *traditionalism* and *modernism*, Ray calls this group the *integral culture*. Exactly how "integral" this group is remains to be seen; but I believe Ray's figures indeed represent a series of very real currents. The traditionalists are grounded in premodern mythic values (blue); the modernists, in rational-industrial values (orange); and the cultural creatives, in postformal/postmodern values (green). Those three movements constitute exactly what we would expect from our survey of the development and evolution of consciousness (preformal mythic to formal rational to early postformal).

But a few more points stand out. What Ray calls the integral culture is not integral as I am using the term; it is not grounded in universal integralism, mature vision-logic, or second-tier consciousness. Rather, as Ray's survey results suggest, the majority of cultural creatives are basically *activating the green meme*, as their values clearly indicate: strongly antihierarchical; concerned with dialogue; embracing a flatland holism ("holistic everything," as Ray puts it, except that all genuine holism involves nested hierarchy, or holarchy, and the cultural creatives eschew holarchy, so their holism is usually an amalgam of monological wholeness claims, such as offered by physics or systems theory); suspicious of conventional forms of most everything; admirably sensitive to the marginalization of minorities; committed to pluralistic values and subjectivistic warrants; and possessing a largely translative, not transformative, spirituality.[8] As Don Beck himself points out, using substantial research, "Ray's 'integral culture' is essentially the green meme. There are few if any indications of yellow or turquoise memes; in other words, there are few second-tier memes in most of the cultural creatives."[9]

Further empirical research strongly supports this interpretation. Ray claims that 24 percent of Americans are cultural creatives in an integral culture. I believe he has accurately measured something, but it is actually the fact that most cultural creatives, to use Jane Loevinger and Susanne Cook-Greuter's terms, are at the *individualistic* stage (green), not the *autonomous* or *integrated* stages (yellow and turquoise). Research shows that, indeed, less than 2 percent of Americans are at the autonomous or integrated stage (this also fits very closely with Beck's research—less than 2 percent at second tier—as well as with that of most other developmentalists). In short, the cultural creatives, most of whom are boomers, are not truly integral, but are basically activating the green meme.[10]

In fact, since it is the green meme that, if not let go of, is what immediately prevents the emergence of second-tier integration, what Paul Ray calls the "integral culture" is actually what is *preventing* the integral culture.

Almost any way we slice the data, the "integral culture" is not that integral.

But it can be. And that is the crucial point. As the cultural creatives move into the second half of life, this is exactly the time that a further transformation of consciousness, from green into mature second-tier awareness, can most easily occur. As I will later suggest, this transformation into second-tier integral consciousness (and higher, into genuinely transpersonal waves) can most readily be effected by *integral transformative practice*. The only reason I am talking about "boomeritis" is with the hope that, by discussing some of the obstacles to this further transformation, it might more readily occur.

These obstacles are not found exclusively in boomers or in Americans. Pluralistic relativism is a universally available wave of consciousness unfolding, and it has its own perils and stick-points, of which intense subjectivism, magnet for narcissism, is a major one. Thus "boomeritis" is by no means confined to boomers, but can afflict anybody poised for the leap into second-tier consciousness, itself the great gateway to more enduring spiritual and transpersonal awareness.

We can now turn to that more integral vision.

3

An Integral Vision

Make everything as simple as possible, but not simpler.
— ALBERT EINSTEIN

INTEGRAL TRANSFORMATION

IT APPEARS, then, that approximately 1–2 percent of the population is at an integral, second-tier stance, but that around 20 percent are at green, poised for that possible integral transformation, for that "momentous leap," as Clare Graves called it.

What are the conditions that can help facilitate that transformation? Developmental theorists have isolated dozens of factors that contribute to vertical transformation (as opposed to horizontal translation). In my own view, catalytic factors from several dimensions need to be present in order for transformation to occur.[1]

To begin with, the individual must possess an organic structure (including brain structure) that can support such a reorganization. For most people, this is not a problem. At this point in evolution, most individuals are biologically capable of integral consciousness.

The cultural background must be ready to support such a transformation, or, at the very least, not dramatically oppose it. Even thirty years ago, this might have been a problem. But numerous factors indicate that there is now a *cultural readiness* for a more integral embrace. To begin with, we have had three decades of the green meme as a substantial percentage of the population, and it has mightily tilled the soil for such a transformation (at least among the green-meme population itself, or among some 40 million Americans;

research indicates that approximately the same percentage of the population in Europe is also at green; see fig. 6-2, p. 119). That, in fact, is what Clare Graves said was the major function of green; namely, to make the entire Spiral *sensitive* (the sensitive self) and thus ready it for second-tier transformation.

But in order for this to happen, consciousness must go post-green. Paraphrasing Graves, "The green meme must break down in order to free energy for the jump into second-tier. This is where the leading edge is today."[2] Since the major cause of fixation to the green meme is boomeritis, then in order for this integral transformation to readily occur, boomeritis must be addressed and remedied, at least to a substantial degree. (Suggestions for doing so are set forth in *Boomeritis*.) But the fact is, if you see the problem of boomeritis and recognize its dangers, you are already over that hump.

As for the concrete social institutions and techno-economic base contributing to transformation, there need to be profound technological advances in one or more areas, advances that impose a pressure on individual consciousness. (This, of course, is an old Marxist argument: when the forces of production run ahead of the relations of production, wrenching cultural transformations ensue. This is a partial truth of Marxism that has not been discredited.)

We have recently had several such techno-economic shifts, including preeminently the microchip/digital revolution. That this is the "information age," and that this constitutes one of the half-dozen major social transformations in history (foraging, horticultural, agrarian, industrial, informational) is so widely known and accepted that we needn't dwell further on it. All we need note is that global communications have made global and integral consciousness a widespread possibility. This global network of technology, this new nervous system for collective consciousness, does not, however, in any way guarantee that individuals will in fact develop to an integral level in their own case. It *facilitates*, but does *not* guarantee. Moreover, global or planetary does not necessarily mean integral. After all, red memes can use the Internet, blue memes can use the Internet, orange memes can use the Internet, and so on. The level or stage of consciousness is determined by *interior factors* (which we will discuss next), and not merely by exterior structures, no matter how planetary or global.

We come, then, to the last dimension—that of individual consciousness itself—and the factors that facilitate personal transformation (given that the other factors are more or less in place). There are four factors that I think are particularly important: fulfillment, dissonance, insight, and opening.

Fulfillment means that the individual has generally fulfilled the basic tasks of a given stage or wave. A basic competence has been established at that level. The person does not have to perfectly master a given level or stage, but simply function adequately enough to move forward. If the person does not do so, then *developmental arrest* sets in and further transformation is unlikely. There is a more subjective way to put this: individuals need to fully taste a given stage, get their fill of it, and thus be ready to move on. A person still hungry for the particular food of a given stage will simply not look elsewhere.

On the other hand, if the person has tasted a stage and become fairly full, then he or she is open to transformation. In order for this to occur, some sort of *dissonance* generally has to set in. The new wave is struggling to emerge, the old wave is struggling to hang on, and the individual feels torn, feels dissonance, feels pulled in several directions. But in any event there has to be some sort of profound dissatisfaction with the present level; one has to be agitated, annoyed, frustrated with it, so that a deep and conflicted dissonance insistently arises. (One of the reasons I wrote *Boomeritis* was to generate some sort of genuine dissonance in the green meme. This has not, on balance, endeared me to greens, but there it is.)

In any event, one has to be willing to let go of—or die to—the present level. Perhaps one has run up against its inherent limitations or contradictions (as Hegel would say), or one is beginning to disidentify with it (as Assagioli explained), or perhaps one has just gotten tired of it. At this point, some sort of *insight* into the situation—insight into what one actually wants, and insight into what reality actually offers—usually helps the individual to move forward. Affirmation, volition, and the intention to change can all be parts of insight into the situation, helping to drive consciousness forward. This insight can be facilitated by introspection, by conversations with friends, by therapy, by meditation, or—more often than not, and in ways that absolutely nobody understands—by simply living.

Finally, if all of those factors fall into place, then an *opening* to the next wave of consciousness—deeper, higher, wider, more encompassing—becomes possible.

Thus, when it comes to the integral wave, what individuals who are already poised for an integral transformation—who already have tasted green to the full and are ready to move on, who already feel some sort of dissonance with their present state, who already are looking for something deeper, wider, more meaningful—can do to facilitate this "momentous leap" in their own case can be summarized in two parts: we need an *integral vision*, and we need an *integral practice*. The integral vision helps provide us with insight, and thus helps us overcome dissonance and face toward our own deeper and wider opening. And integral practice anchors all of these factors in a concrete manner, so that they do not remain merely abstract ideas and vague notions.

Let us also note that, as one's consciousness begins to find a home in second tier, a genuine Theory of Everything becomes a startling possibility. At the very least, it becomes deeply appealing, speaking as it does to the inherent holism of second-tier embrace.

In the next few chapters, I will outline one version of an integral vision or T.O.E., and explore its usefulness in everything from integral medicine to integral business to integral politics to integral spirituality. (I am not saying that this is the only type of integral vision possible, or even the best. But it is the best that I am aware of; if I knew a better one, I would present that.) Once we have a general grasp of this integral vision—a general overview of a Theory of Everything—we will look specifically at what might constitute an effective integral practice, so that, should you desire, you can make integral awareness a living reality in your own case, and thus bring a more comprehensive approach to the many ways that we can try to help others.

Sex, Ecology, Spirituality

I first attempted to outline this T.O.E. in a book called *Sex, Ecology, Spirituality* (SES). Since I am often asked about the book's genesis, how and why I came to write it, and the critical responses to it, let me interrupt this theoretical narrative with a personal account of each of those items.

SES was the first book I had written in almost ten years, following the events described in *Grace and Grit: Spirituality and Healing in the Life and Death of Treya Killam Wilber*. (Ten days after Treya and I were married, in 1983, she was diagnosed with breast cancer.

We spent the next five years fighting that disease. Treya died in 1989, at the age of 41. She asked me to write of our ordeal; *Grace and Grit* was the result.)

The previous book, *Transformations of Consciousness* (with Jack Engler and Daniel P. Brown), was completed in 1984; I wrote *Grace and Grit* in 1991; and then I settled down to finally write a textbook of integral psychology that I had been planning on doing for several years. I was calling that textbook *System, Self, and Structure*, but somehow it never seemed to get written. Determined to complete it, I sat down and begin transcribing the two-volume work, whereupon I realized, with a shock, that four of the words I used in the very first paragraph were no longer allowed in academic discourse (development, hierarchy, transcendental, universal). This, needless to say, put a considerable cramp in my attempt to write this book, and poor *System, Self, and Structure* was, yet again, shelved. (I recently brought out an abridged version with the title *Integral Psychology*.)

What had happened in my ten-year writing hiatus, and to which I had paid insufficient attention, is that extreme postmodernism and the green meme had rather completely invaded academia in general and cultural studies in particular—even the alternative colleges and institutes were speaking postmodernese with an authoritarian thunder. The politically correct were policing the types of serious discourse that could, and could not, be uttered in academe. Pluralistic relativism was the only acceptable worldview. It claimed that all truth is culturally situated (except its own truth, which is true for all cultures); it claimed there are no transcendental truths (except its own pronouncements, which transcend specific contexts); it claimed that all hierarchies or value rankings are oppressive and marginalizing (except its own value ranking, which is superior to the alternatives); it claimed that there are no universal truths (except its own pluralism, which is universally true for all peoples).

The downsides of extreme postmodernism and pluralistic relativism are now well-known and widely acknowledged, but at the time I was trying to write *System, Self, and Structure*, they were thought to be gospel and were as religiously embraced, making any sort of developmental and transcendental studies anathema. I therefore set *System, Self, and Structure* aside and began to ponder how to continue, feeling rather like a salmon who had first to swim upstream in order to have any fun at all.

One thing was very clear to me, as I struggled with how best to proceed in an intellectual climate dedicated to deconstructing anything that crossed its path: I would have to back up and start at the beginning, and try to create a vocabulary for a more constructive philosophy. Beyond pluralistic relativism is universal integralism; I therefore sought to outline a philosophy of universal integralism.

Put differently, I sought a world philosophy—or an *integral* philosophy—that would believably weave together the many pluralistic contexts of science, morals, aesthetics, Eastern as well as Western philosophy, and the world's great wisdom traditions. Not on the level of details—that is finitely impossible; but on the level of *orienting generalizations*: a way to suggest that the world really is one, undivided, whole, and related to itself in every way: a holistic philosophy for a holistic Kosmos, a plausible Theory of Everything.

Three years later, *Sex, Ecology, Spirituality* was the result. During that period I lived the hermit life; I saw exactly four people in three years (Roger Walsh, who is an M.D., stopped by once a year to make sure I was alive); it was very much a typical three-year silent retreat (this period is described in *One Taste*, June 12 entry). I was locked into this thing, and it would not let go.

The hard part had to do with *hierarchies*. Granted, dominator hierarchies are deplorable, and oppressive social rankings are pernicious. Postmodernism has fortunately made us all more sensitive to those injustices. But even the antihierarchy critics have their own strong hierarchies (or value rankings). The postmodernists value pluralism over absolutism—and that is their value hierarchy. Even the eco-philosophers, who abhor hierarchies that place humans on the top of the evolutionary scale, have their own very strong hierarchy, which is: subatomic elements are parts of atoms, which are parts of molecules, which are parts of cells, which are parts of organisms, which are parts of ecosystems, which are parts of the biosphere. They thus value the biosphere above particular organisms, such as man, and they deplore man's using the biosphere for his own selfish and ruinous purposes. All of that comes from their particular value hierarchy.

Feminists have several hierarchies (e.g., partnership societies are better than power societies; linking is better than ranking; liberation is better than oppression); systems theorists have hundreds of hierarchies (most natural systems are arranged hierarchically); biologists and linguists and developmental psychologists all have hierarchies. (Even those memes that don't recognize hierarchies—such as beige or purple—still have hierarchical structures). *Everybody* seemed to have some sort of hierarchy, even those who claimed they didn't. The problem is, none of them matched with the others. None of the hierarchies seemed to agree with each other. And that was the basic problem that kept me locked in my room for three years.

At one point, I had over two hundred hierarchies written out on legal pads lying all over the floor, trying to figure out how to fit them together. There were the "natural science" hierarchies, which were the easy ones, since everybody agreed with them: atoms to molecules to cells to organisms, for example. They were easy to understand because they were so graphic: organisms actually contain cells, which actually contain molecules, which actually contain atoms. You can even see this directly with a microscope. That hierarchy is one of actual embrace: cells literally embrace or enfold molecules.

The other fairly easy series of hierarchies were those discovered by the developmental psychologists. They all told variations on the hierarchy that goes from preconventional to conventional to post-conventional, or in a bit more detail, from sensation to perception to impulse to image to symbol to concept to rule to formal. . . . The names varied, and the schemes were slightly different, but the hierarchical story was the same—each succeeding stage incorporated its predecessors and then added some new capacity. This seemed very similar to the natural science hierarchies, except they still did not match up in any obvious way. Moreover, you can actually see organisms and cells in the empirical world, but you can't see interior states of consciousness in the same way. It is not at all obvious how these hierarchies would—or even could—be related.

And those were the easy ones. There were linguistic hierarchies, contextual hierarchies, spiritual hierarchies. There were stages of development in phonetics, stellar systems, cultural worldviews, auto-poietic systems, technological modes, economic structures, phyloge-netic unfoldings, superconscious realizations. . . . And they simply refused to agree with each other.

G. Spencer Brown, in his remarkable book, *Laws of Form*, said that new knowledge comes when you simply bear in mind what you need to know. Keep holding the problem in mind, and it will yield. The history of human beings is certainly testament to that fact. An individual runs into a problem, and simply obsesses about that problem until he or she solves it. And the funny thing is: the prob-lem is always solved. Sooner or later, it yields. It might take a week, a month, a year, a decade, a century, or a millennium, but the Kosmos appears to be such that solutions are *always* forthcoming. For a million years, humans looked at the moon and wanted to walk on it. . . .

I believe any competent person is capable of bearing problems in mind until they yield their secrets; what not everybody possesses is the requisite will, passion, or insane obsession that will let them hold the problem long enough or fiercely enough. I, at any rate, was insane enough for this particular problem, and toward the end of that three-year period, the whole thing started to become clear to me. It soon became obvious that the various hierarchies fall into four major classes (what I would call the *four quadrants* [see below]); that some of the hierarchies are referring to individuals, some to collectives; some are about exterior realities, some are about interior ones, but they all fit together seamlessly.

The ingredients of these hierarchies are holons. A *holon* is a whole that is a part of other wholes. For example, a whole atom is part of a whole molecule; a whole molecule is part of a whole cell; a whole cell is part of a whole organism. Or again, a whole letter is part of a whole word, which is part of a whole sentence, which is part of a whole paragraph, and so on. Reality is composed of neither wholes nor parts, but of whole/parts, or holons. Reality in all domains is basically composed of holons.

This is also why, as Arthur Koestler pointed out, a growth hierarchy is actually a *holarchy*, since it is composed of holons (such as atoms to molecules to cells to organisms—what we also called nested hierarchy or actualization hierarchy, which is why holarchies are the backbone of holism: they convert heaps to wholes, which are parts of other wholes, limitlessly). The Kosmos is a series of nests within nests within nests indefinitely, expressing greater and greater holistic embrace—holarchies of holons everywhere—which is why *everybody* had their own value holarchy, and why, in the end, all of these holarchies intermesh and fit perfectly with all the others.

The universe is composed of holons, all the way up, all the way down. And with that, much of *Sex, Ecology, Spirituality* began to write itself. The book is divided into two parts (three actually, counting the endnotes, a separate book in themselves). Part One describes this holonic Kosmos—nests within nests within nests indefinitely—and the worldview of universal integralism that I believe can most authentically express it. Part Two attempts to explain why this holistic Kosmos is so often ignored or denied. If the universe really is a pattern of mutually interrelated patterns and processes—holarchies of holons—why do so few disciplines acknowledge this fact? If the Kosmos is *not* holistic, not integral, not holonic—if it is a fragmented and jumbled affair, with no common contexts or linkings or joinings or communions—then fine, the world is the jumbled mess the various specialties take it to be. But if the world is holistic and holonic, then why do not more people see this? And why do many academic specialties actively deny it? If the world is whole, why do so many people see it as broken? And why, in a sense, *is* the world broken, fragmented, alienated, divided?

The second part of the book therefore looks at what prevents us from seeing the holistic Kosmos. It looks at what I call *flatland*. In a sense, flatland is simply the failure to grasp the entire spiral of development or the full spectrum of consciousness; the antidote to flatland is an integral vision, which is what SES attempts to provide.

Once the book was conceived, the actual writing went fairly quickly. It was published in 1995. Reviews ranged from very positive ("Along with Aurobindo's *Life Divine,* Heidegger's *Being and Time,* and Whitehead's *Process and Reality,* Wilber's *Sex, Ecology, Spirituality* is one of the four great books of this century"[3]) to puzzled, confused, or angry ("This is one of the most irritating books of the year, pompous and over-bloated"). But the most common overall reaction to SES was one of what I suppose we might call joy. I was flooded with mail from readers who told of the liberating influence that SES had on their view of the world, on their view of reality, on their consciousness itself. SES is, after all, a story of the feats of your very own Self, and many readers rejoiced at that remembrance. Women forgave me any patriarchal obnoxiousness, men told me of weeping throughout the last chapter. Apart from *Grace and Grit,* I have never received such heartfelt and deeply moving letters as I received from SES, letters that made those difficult three years seem more than worth it.

One critic wrote of SES that "it honors and incorporates more truth than any approach in history." I obviously would like to believe that is the case, but I also know that every tomorrow brings new truths, opens new vistas, and creates the demand for even more encompassing views. SES is simply the latest in a long line of holistic visions, and will itself pass into a greater tomorrow where it is merely a footnote to more glorious views.

In the meantime, I personally believe that SES (and the subsequent books fleshing it out)⁴ can serve as a helpful integral view. *A Brief History of Everything* is a popular version of SES, and interested readers might start there. Of course, it is not necessary that you agree with all of this vision or even most of it—and, in fact, you will probably be able to improve on it, which would be great. This is simply one version of an integral overview—one attempt at a T.O.E.—useful only to the degree that it helps you to envision your own integral possibilities. Shall we take a look?

A FULL-SPECTRUM APPROACH

Let us start with a sketch of an integral map of human possibilities. In the next three sections I will give a simple overview of this integral model as it appears in humans. This brief overview will be a little bit abstract, and if this is not your favorite type of reading, don't worry. In chapters 5 and 6 we will look at many concrete examples in medicine, education, business, politics, and so on. In the meantime, you might simply familiarize yourself with the general ideas, all of which are summarized in a simple fashion in the accompanying diagrams.

Since we have already used Spiral Dynamics as one example of some of the levels or waves of consciousness unfolding, we can continue to use that model, and then plug it into an "all-quadrant, all-level" conception, as shown in figure 3-1.⁵

With reference to figure 3-1, we might note several items. The four quadrants—which will be fully explained in the coming chapters—simply refer to four of the most important dimensions of the Kosmos, namely, the interior and the exterior of the individual and the collective. If you look at figure 4-4 on page 70, you can see a few concrete examples of some of the holons in each of the quadrants. Figure 3-1 is specifically for human holons. In this section we will focus on the *Upper-Left quadrant* in humans (or consciousness in an individual); in the next section, we will look at the other three quadrants.

The Upper-Left quadrant (which is the interior of the individual, and which in the simplistic fig. 3-1 only contains one line and eight levels), actually contains a *full spectrum* of levels (or waves of development—stretching from matter to body to mind to soul to spirit; or again, from archaic to magic to mythic to rational to integral to

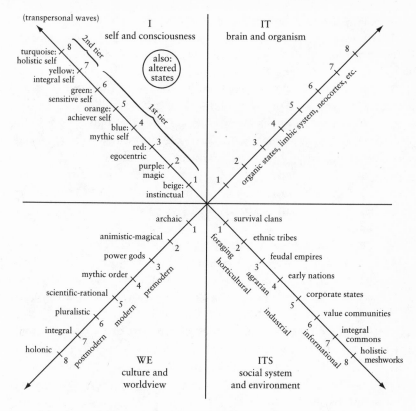

Figure 3-1. Some Examples of the Four Quadrants in Humans

transpersonal, not as rigidly discrete platforms but as overlapping waves); many different *streams* (or *lines* of development—the different modules, dimensions, or areas of development—including cognitive, moral, affective, linguistic, kinesthetic, somatic, interpersonal, etc.); different *states* of consciousness (including waking, dreaming, sleeping, altered, nonordinary, and meditative); and different *types* of consciousness (or possible orientations at every level, including personality types and different gender styles)—all of which will be explained in the following sections—resulting in a richly textured, holodynamic, integral view of consciousness.

Let us focus, for a moment, on waves, streams, and types. *Waves* are the "levels" of development, conceived in a fluid, flowing, and intermeshing fashion, which is how most developmentalists today view them. Figure 3-1 gives eight levels of development; but, as we will see, I believe there are at least four higher, transpersonal, or spiritual waves (psychic, subtle, causal, and nondual). Of course, none of these waves are rigid or linear platforms, like so many bricks stacked on top of each other, but rather are fluid, flowing, average modes of consciousness.

Through these levels or *waves* of development flow many different lines or *streams* of development. We have credible evidence that these different streams, lines, or modules include cognition, morals, self-identity, psychosexuality, ideas of the good, role taking, socio-emotional capacity, creativity, altruism, several lines that can be called "spiritual" (care, openness, concern, religious faith, meditative stages), communicative competence, modes of space and time, affect/emotion, death-seizure, needs, worldviews, mathematical competence, musical skills, kinesthetics, gender identity, defense mechanisms, interpersonal capacity, and empathy.[6]

One of the most striking items about these multiple modules or streams is that most of them develop in a relatively independent fashion. Research is still fleshing out the details of these relationships; some lines are necessary but not sufficient for others; some develop closely together. But on balance, many of the streams develop at their own rate, with their own dynamic, in their own way. A person can be at a relatively high level of development in some streams, medium in others, and low in still others. Overall development, in other words, can be quite uneven.

I have indicated this, in a very simplistic fashion, in figure 3-2. Here the levels of development (or the *levels of consciousness*) are represented on the vertical axis by the Graves/Spiral Dynamic memes.[7] I have added what I believe are three of the higher, transpersonal waves (psychic, subtle, and causal), which we will discuss later.[8] I have also placed the common Christian terms for the full spectrum on the left (matter, body, mind, soul, and spirit), showing their correlations in a very general fashion.

Through those general levels or waves pass various developmental lines or streams. I have selected only five as examples (kinesthetic, cognitive, moral, emotional, and spiritual), but you can see the uneven development that is theoretically possible (and that empirical research has continued to confirm often happens).

Since the waves of development are actually a *holarchy*, this can also be indicated in as in figure 3-3. Here, I am using just four major levels—body, mind, soul, and spirit, each of which transcends and includes its predecessors in increasing waves of integral embrace (a

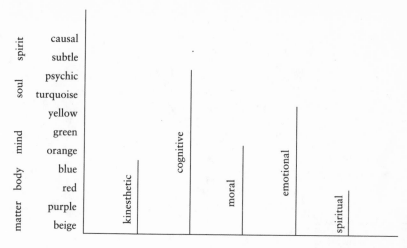

Figure 3-2. Waves and Streams

true holarchy of nests within nests). And since most lines of development are not linear but are also a fluid, flowing, spiraling affair, figure 3-3 is actually more accurately represented as in figure 3-4. But all of these figures show the uneven, nonlinear nature of most development.

This model sheds considerable light on the fact that, for example, some individuals—including spiritual teachers—may be highly evolved in certain capacities (such as meditative awareness or cognitive brilliance), and yet demonstrate poor (or even pathological) development in other streams, such as the psychosexual or interpersonal.

This also allows us to spot the ways in which the spiritual traditions themselves—from shamanism to Buddhism to Christianity to indigenous religions—might excel in training certain lines or capacities, but fall short in many others, or even be pathological in many others. A more integral transformative practice might therefore seek a more balanced or "all-quadrant, all-level" approach to transformation (see below).

As for *types*, see figure 3-5, which uses the enneagram as an example. What I have done here is take only one developmental line (it can be anything—morals, cognition, etc.) and list the levels or waves of development through which this particular stream will tend to unfold (using Spiral Dynamics as an example of the waves). At each level I have drawn the enneagram as an example of what might be called a *horizontal* typology, or a typology of the personality types

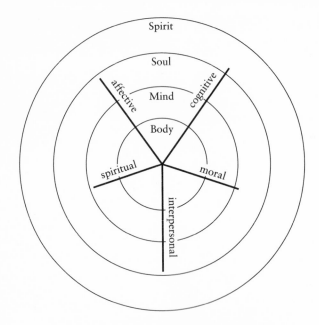

Figure 3-3. The Holarchy of Development

that can exist at almost any vertical level of development. The point is that a person can be a particular *type* (using Jungian types, Myers-Briggs, the enneagram, etc.) at virtually any of the levels. Thus, if a person is, say, predominantly enneagram type 5, then as they develop they would be purple 5, red 5, blue 5, and so on (again, not in a rigid linear fashion, but in a fluid and flowing mesh).[9]

For many feminists, *male and female orientations* also constitute a type. Based mostly on work by Carol Gilligan and Deborah Tannen, the idea is that the typical male orientation tends to be more agentic, autonomous, abstract, and independent, based on rights and justice; whereas the female orientation tends to be more permeable, relational, and feelingful, based on care and responsibility. Gilligan, recall, agrees that females proceed through three (or four) hierarchical stages of development, and these are essentially the same three (or four) hierarchical stages or waves through which males proceed (namely, preconventional, conventional, postconventional, and integrated).

The reason that many people, especially feminists, still incorrectly believe that Gilligan denied a female hierarchy of development is that Gilligan found that males tend to make judgments using ranking or

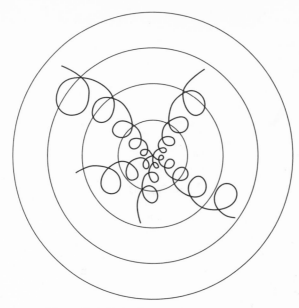

Figure 3-4. Spiraling Streams and Waves

hierarchical thinking, whereas women tend to make judgments using linking or relational thinking (what I summarize as agency and communion, respectively). But what many people overlooked is that Gilligan maintained that the *female orientation itself proceeds through three (or four) hierarchical stages*—from selfish to care to universal care to integrated. Thus, many feminists confused the idea that females tend not to think hierarchically with the idea that females do not develop hierarchically; the former is true, the latter is false, according to Gilligan herself.[10] (Why was Gilligan so widely misread and distorted in this area? Because the green meme denies hierarchies in general, and thus it literally could not perceive her message accurately.)

In *The Eye of Spirit* (chap. 8, "Integral Feminism"), I summarize this research by saying that men and women both proceed through the same general waves of development, but men tend to do so with an emphasis on agency, women with an emphasis on communion.[11]

This approach to gender development allows us to utilize the extensive contributions of developmental studies, but also supplement them with a keener understanding of how females evolve "in a different voice" through the great waves of existence. In the past, it was not uncommon to find orthodox psychological researchers

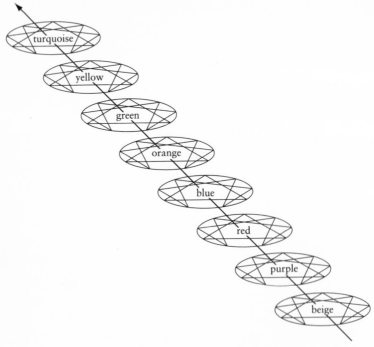

Figure 3-5. Levels and Types

defining females as "deficient males" (i.e., females "lack" logic, rationality, a sense of justice; they are even defined by "penis envy," or desiring that which they lack). Nowadays it is not uncommon to find, especially among feminists, the reverse prejudice: males are defined as "deficient females" (i.e., males "lack" sensitivity, care, relational capacity, embodiment, etc.).

Well, we might say, a plague on both houses. With this more integral approach, we can trace development through the great waves and streams of existence, but also recognize that males and females might navigate that great River of Life using a different style, type, or voice. This means that we can still recognize the major waves of existence—which, in fact, are gender-neutral—but we must fully honor the validity of *both* styles of navigating those waves.[12]

Finally, individuals at virtually any stage of development can have an *altered state* or *peak experience*, including those that are called spiritual experiences, and this can have a profound effect on their consciousness and its development. Thus, the idea that spiritual experiences can only occur at higher stages is incorrect. However, in order for altered *states* to become permanent *traits*, they need to enter the stream of enduring development.[13]

The point is that, even looking at just the Upper-Left quadrant, a more integral map of consciousness is now at least possible, one that includes waves, streams, states, and types, all of which appear to be important ingredients in this extraordinary spectrum of consciousness.

All-Quadrant

But individual or subjective consciousness does not exist in a vacuum; no subject is an island unto itself. Individual consciousness is inextricably intermeshed with the objective organism and brain (Upper-Right quadrant); with nature, social systems, and environment (Lower-Right quadrant); and with cultural settings, communal values, and worldviews (Lower-Left quadrant). Again, each of these quadrants has numerous waves, streams, and types, only a pitifully few of which are indicated in fig. 3-1. In books such as *A Brief History of Everything*, *The Eye of Spirit*, and *Integral Psychology*, I have given a wide variety of examples from each quadrant, as they relate to art and literary interpretation, feminism and gender studies, anthropology, philosophy, psychology, and religion. Here are a few quick examples:

The Upper-Right quadrant is the individual viewed in an objective, empirical, "scientific" fashion. In particular, this includes organic body states, biochemistry, neurobiological factors, neurotransmitters, organic brain structures (brain stem, limbic system, neocortex), and so on. Whatever we might think about the actual relation of mind-consciousness (Upper Left) and brain-body (Upper Right), we can at least agree they are intimately related. The point is simply that an "all-quadrant, all-level" model would certainly include the important correlations of waves, streams, states, and types of consciousness (UL) with brain states, organic substrates, neurotransmitters, and so on (UR).

There is now occurring an extraordinary amount of research into organic brain states and their relation to consciousness—so much so that most orthodox researchers tend to simply *reduce* consciousness to brain mechanisms. But this reductionism devastates the contours of consciousness itself, reduces "I" experiences to "it" systems, and denies the phenomenal realities of the interior domains altogether. The insidiousness of this reduction of Upper Left to Upper Right is avoided when we take instead an all-quadrant, all-level approach, which refuses unwarrantedly to reduce any level, line, or quadrant to any other.[14]

The Lower-Left quadrant involves all those patterns in consciousness that are shared by those who are "in" a particular culture or subculture. For you and I to understand each other at all, we need, at the very least, to share certain linguistic semantics, numerous perceptions, worldviews that overlap to some degree (so that communication is possible at all), and so on. These shared values, perceptions, meanings, semantic habitats, cultural practices, ethics, and so on, I simply refer to as *culture*, or the *intersubjective* patterns in consciousness.

These cultural perceptions, all of which exist to some degree in ntersubjective spaces in consciousness, nonetheless have *objective* correlates that can be empirically detected—physical structures and institutions, including techno-economic modes (foraging, horticultural, maritime, agrarian, industrial, informational), architectural styles, geopolitical structures, modes of information transfer (vocal signs, ideograms, movable type printing, telecommunications, microchip), social structure (survival clans, ethnic tribes, feudal - orders, ancient nations, corporate states, value communities, and so on). I refer to these *interobjective* realities in general as the *social system* (the Lower-Right quadrant).

Figure 3-6 depicts the fact that, throughout history, different theorists have often focused on one quadrant, often to the exclusion of others. The "Right-Hand Paths" have all focused on the exterior quadrants—those items that can be seen with the senses or their extensions. Theorists and researchers of the Upper Right focus on the *exterior* of *individuals*—behaviorism, empiricism, physics, biology, cognitive science, neurology, brain physiology, and so on. (Even though the brain is on the inside of the organism, it is investigated in an objective, exterior, scientific fashion, and hence is part of the Upper Right.) The Upper-Right quadrant is what we most often think of as the hard sciences.

Theorists of the Lower Right focus on the *exterior* of the *collective*, or the systems sciences—systems theory, the ecological web of life, chaos and complexity theories, techno-economic structures, environmental networks, and social systems. Both of the Right-Hand quadrants are approached in objective, third-person, "it" language, and thus both are usually thought of as "scientific" (the UR being individual sciences and the LR being systems sciences). [15]

The "Left-Hand Paths" all focus on the *interior* quadrants. Theorists and researchers of the Upper Left investigate interior consciousness as it appears in *individuals,* and this has resulted in everything from psychoanalysis to phenomenology to introspective psychology to meditative states of consciousness (e.g., Freud to Jung to Piaget to Buddha). These phenomenal realities are all expressed, not in "it" language but in "I" language (not third person but first person).

Theorists of the Lower Left investigate the *interior* of the *collective*—all the shared values, perceptions, worldviews, and background cultural contexts that are expressed, not in "I" language or

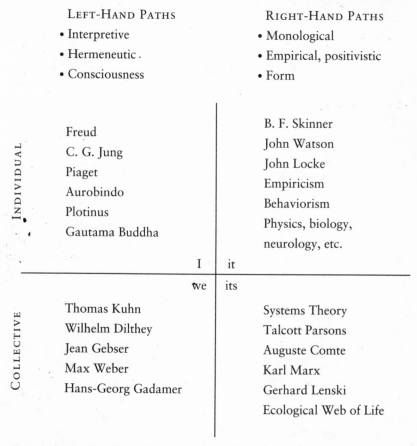

LEFT-HAND PATHS	RIGHT-HAND PATHS
• Interpretive	• Monological
• Hermeneutic.	• Empirical, positivistic
• Consciousness	• Form

INDIVIDUAL

Freud	B. F. Skinner
C. G. Jung	John Watson
Piaget	John Locke
Aurobindo	Empiricism
Plotinus	Behaviorism
Gautama Buddha	Physics, biology, neurology, etc.
I	it
we	its

COLLECTIVE

Thomas Kuhn	Systems Theory
Wilhelm Dilthey	Talcott Parsons
Jean Gebser	Auguste Comte
Max Weber	Karl Marx
Hans-Georg Gadamer	Gerhard Lenski
	Ecological Web of Life

Figure 3-6. Some Representative Theorists in Each Quadrant

in "it" language, but in "we" language. These theorists include the hermeneutic, interpretive, and phenomenological cultural studies (such as Thomas Kuhn and Jean Gebser). The profound effects of background cultural contexts on the other quadrants have especially been emphasized by the various postmodern writers (from Nietzsche to Heidegger to Foucault to Derrida), even if they overstate the case.

As you will see in the following pages, the integral approach that I am recommending—and which I simplistically summarize as "all-quadrant, all-level"—is dedicated to including all of the nonreducible realities in all of the quadrants, which means all of the waves, streams, states, and types, as disclosed by reputable, nonreductionistic researchers. All four quadrants, with all their realities, mutually interact and evolve—they "tetra-interact" and "tetra-evolve"—and a more integral approach is sensitive to those richly textured patterns of infinite interaction.

I sometimes simplify this model even further by calling it a "1-2-3" approach to the Kosmos. This refers to first-person, second-person, and third-person realities. As I briefly mentioned (and as you can see in figs. 3-1 and 3-6), the Upper-Left quadrant involves "I-language" (or first-person accounts); the Lower-Left quadrant involves "we-language" (or second-person accounts); and both Right-Hand quadrants, since they are objective patterns, involve "it-language" (or third-person accounts).[16]

Thus, the four quadrants can be simplified to the "Big Three" (I, we, and it). These important dimensions can be stated in many different ways: art, morals, and science; the Beautiful, the Good, and the True; self, culture, and nature. The point of an "all-quadrant, all-level" approach is that it would honor all of the waves of existence—from body to mind to soul to spirit—as they all unfold in self, culture, and nature.

Simplest of all, I refer to this model as "holonic." As we saw, a holon is a whole that is a part of other wholes. A whole atom is part of a whole molecule; a whole molecule is part of a whole cell; a whole cell is part of a whole organism. Reality is composed of neither wholes nor parts, but whole/parts, or holons. The fundamental entities in all of the quadrants, levels, and lines are simply holons (see SES for a full elaboration of this topic). As Arthur Koestler pointed out, a growth hierarchy is actually a holarchy, since it is composed of holons (such as atoms to molecules to cells to organisms). This is why the only way you get a holism is via a holarchy, and why those who deny all hierarchies have only a heapism, not a wholism.

There is a nice symmetry here, in that Beck and Cowan specifically refer to second-tier thinking as recognizing and operating with "holons." As they put it, second tier is defined as "Holon: Everything flows with everything else in living systems; second tier stitches together particles, people, functions and nodes into networks and stratified levels [nested hierarchies or holarchies], and detects the energy fields that engulf, billow around, and flow throughout naturally in a 'big picture' of cosmic order." That "big picture" is a T.O.E., and that order appears to be holonic. . . .

A MORE INTEGRAL MAP

What, then, can we say about a more integral model of human possibilities? Before we can talk about *applications* of an integral vision—in education, politics, business, health care, and so on—we need to have some general notion of what it is that we are applying in the first place. When we move from pluralistic relativism to universal integralism, what kind of map might we find? We have seen that a more integral cartography might include:

- multiple levels or *waves* of existence, a grand holarchy spanning the entire spectrum of consciousness, matter to body to mind to soul to spirit (or beige to purple to red to blue to orange to . . . subtle, causal, nondual). Moving through those levels of development, there are
- numerous different *streams*, modules, or lines of development, including cognitive, moral, spiritual, aesthetic, somatic, imaginative, interpersonal, and so on (e.g., one can be cognitive orange, emotional purple, moral blue, and so forth). Moreover, at virtually any stage of development, one is open to
- multiple *states* of consciousness, including waking, dreaming, sleeping, altered, nonordinary, and meditative (many of these altered states can occur at any level; thus, for example, one can have a variety of religious experiences at virtually any stage of development).[17]
- numerous different *types* of consciousness, including gender

types, personality types (enneagram, Myers–Briggs, Jungian), and so on. These types can occur in levels, lines, and states.

- multiple organic factors and brain states (this Upper-Right quadrant today receives most of the attention from psychiatry, cognitive science, and neurobiology; but as significant as it is, it is still only "one-fourth" of the story).

- the extraordinarily important impact of numerous *cultural* factors, including the rich textures of diverse cultural realities, background contexts, pluralistic perceptions, linguistic semantics, and so on, none of which should be unwarrantedly marginalized, all of which should be included and integrated in a broad web of integral-aperspectival tapestries. (And, just as important, a truly "integral transformative practice" would give considerable weight to the importance of relationships, community, culture, and intersubjective factors in general, not merely as a realm of application of spiritual insight, but as a means of spiritual transformation).

- the massively influential forces of the *social* system, at all levels (from nature to human structures, including especially the techno-economic base, as well as the profoundly important relationship with nonhuman social systems, from Gaia to ecosystems).

- although I have not mentioned it in this simple overview, the importance of the self as the navigator of the great River of Life should not be overlooked. It appears that the self is not a monolithic entity but rather a society of selves with a *center of gravity*, which acts to bind the multiple waves, states, streams, and realms into something of a unified organization; the disruption of this organization, at any of its general stages, can result in pathology.[18]

Such are a few of the multiple factors that a richly holonic view of the Kosmos might wish to include. At the very least, any model that does not *coherently* include most of those items is not a very integral model. Much of my writing has been dedicated to trying to present the reader with the conclusions from researchers working with second-tier conceptions, whether from premodern, modern, or postmodern sources. Researchers, that is, who are looking at the entire spectrum of consciousness, in all its many waves, streams, states, and realms. And, beyond that, to present an all-quadrant, all-level view, which is the full spectrum in its multiple modalities—a conception that specifically attempts to accommodate the most amount of evidence from the most number of researchers.

As I said, the above overview is a bit dry and abstract, simply because we had to cover much ground in a short space. In subsequent chapters we will see many concrete examples of these ideas, whereupon they will, I trust, become more alive and vibrant.

This integrative attempt points up exactly what I believe is the central issue for cultural and integral studies at the millennium: will we remain stuck in the green meme—with both its wonderful contributions (e.g., pluralistic sensitivity) and its pathologies (e.g., boomeritis)? Or will we make the leap to the hyperspace of second-tier consciousness, and thus stand open to even further evolution into the transpersonal waves of our own possibilities?

To Change the Mapmaker

One of the questions we are dealing with, in other words, is how to more effectively implement the emergence of integral (and even transpersonal) consciousness at the leading edge. What is required, in my opinion, is not simply a new integral theory or a new T.O.E., important as that is, but also a new *integral practice*. Even if we possessed the perfect integral map of the Kosmos, a map that was completely all-inclusive and unerringly holistic, that map itself would not transform people. We don't just need a map; we need ways to change the mapmaker.

Thus, although most of my books attempt to offer a genuinely integral vision, they almost always end with a call for some sort of integral practice—a practice that exercises body, mind, soul, and spirit in self, culture, and nature (all-level, all-quadrant). You will hear this call constantly in the following pages, along with specific suggestions for how to begin a truly integral transformative practice in your own case, if such seems desirable to you.

The Prime Directive

The applications of this holonic model—in education, spiritual practice, politics, business, health care, and so on—will be explored in chapters 5 and 6. In the meantime, let us return to our major points —the impact of an integral vision on both the leading edge and the average mode—and note the following.

One of the main conclusions of an all-quadrant, all-level approach is that each meme—each level of consciousness and wave of existence—is, in its healthy form, *an absolutely necessary and desirable element* of the overall spiral, of the overall spectrum of consciousness. Even if every society on earth were established fully at second tier, nonetheless every infant born in every society still has to start at level 1, at beige, at sensorimotor instincts and perceptions, and then must grow and evolve through purple magic, red and blue myth, orange rationalism, green sensitivity, and into yellow and turquoise second tier (on the way to the transpersonal). All of those waves have important tasks and functions; all of them are taken up and included in subsequent waves; none of them can be bypassed; and none of them can be demeaned without grave consequences to self and society. *The health of the entire spiral is the prime directive, not preferential treatment for any one level.*

A More Measured Greatness

Because the health of the entire spectrum of consciousness is paramount, and not any particular level, this means that a genuinely universal integralism would measure more carefully its actual impact. I believe that the real revolutions facing today's world involve, not a glorious collective move into transpersonal domains, but the simple, fundamental changes that can be brought to the magic, mythic, and rational waves of existence.

Human beings are born and begin their evolution through the great spiral of consciousness, moving from archaic to magic to mythic to rational to perhaps integral, and from there perhaps into genuinely transpersonal domains. But for every person that moves into integral or higher, dozens are born into the archaic. The spiral of existence is a great unending flow, stretching from body to mind to soul to spirit, with millions upon millions constantly flowing through that great river from source to ocean. No society will ever simply be *at* an integral level, because the flow is unceasing (although the center of gravity of a culture can indeed drift upward, as it has over history— see *Up from Eden*). But the major problem remains: not, how can we get everybody to the integral wave or higher, but how can we arrange *the health of the overall spiral*, as billions of humans continue to pass through it, from one end to the other, year in and year out?

In other words, most of the work that needs to be done is work to make the lower (and foundational) waves more healthy in their own terms. The major reforms do not involve how to get a handful of boomers into second tier, but how to feed the starving millions at the most basic waves; how to house the homeless millions at the simplest of levels; how to bring health care to the millions who do not possess it. An integral vision is one of the least pressing issues on the face of the planet.

The Integral Vision in the World at Large

Let me drive this point home using calculations done by Dr. Phillip Harter of Stanford University School of Medicine. If we could shrink the earth's population to a village of only 100 people, it would look something like this:

There would be

- 57 Asians
- 21 Europeans
- 14 North and South Americans
- 8 Africans
- 30 white
- 70 nonwhite
- 6 people would possess 59% of the world's wealth, and all 6 would be from the United States
- 80 would live in substandard housing
- 70 would be unable to read
- 50 would suffer malnutrition
- 1 would have a college education
- 1 would own a computer

Thus, as I suggested, an integral vision is one of the least pressing issues on the face of the planet. The health of the entire spiral, and particularly its earlier waves, screams out to us as the major ethical demand.

Nonetheless, the advantage of second-tier integral awareness is that it more creatively helps with the solutions to those pressing problems. In grasping big pictures, it can help suggest more cogent solutions. It is our governing bodies, then, that stand in dire need of a more integral approach. It is our educational institutions, overcome with deconstructive postmodernism, that are desperate for a more integral vision. It is our business practices, saturated with fragmented gains, that cry out for a more balanced approach. It is our health-care facilities that could greatly benefit from the tender mercies of an integral touch. It is the leadership of the nations that might appreciate a more comprehensive vision of their own possibilities. In all these ways and more, we could indeed use an integral vision for a world gone slightly mad.

4

Science and Religion

Science without religion is lame, religion without science is blind.

— ALBERT EINSTEIN

S CIENCE AND RELIGION, science and religion, science and religion. Their relationship really would drive humanity insane, if only humanity were sensitive enough. As it is, their relationship is merely fated to be one of those damnable dyads—like mind and body, consciousness and matter, facts and values—that remain annoying thorns in philosophers' sides. Ordinary men and women, on the other hand, have always drawn freely on both science (or some sort of technical-empirical knowledge) and religion (or some sort of meaning, value, transcendental purpose, or immanent presence). Still, how to fit them together: "Ah, and there's the rub," as Shakespeare put it.

One thing is certain: any truly integral vision or T.O.E. will have to reconcile, one way or another, the relation of science and religion.

In several books I have specifically addressed this delicate issue.[1] I believe these books are advancing points that are not getting a hearing in the typical debates on science and spirituality (points I will summarize below). I also suspect that these points will, for the most part, continue to be neglected, because they champion a direct experience of Spirit, and not simply ideas about Spirit. In other words, I am attempting to include direct contemplative and experiential spirituality in this debate, whereas most writers on the topic simply want to discuss the philosophical or scientific ideas involved: not direct experience but abstractions. It is as if a group of scholars were discussing the beaches of Hawaii, and instead of going to Hawaii and looking for themselves, they simply pulled out a bunch of geography books and studied them. They study the maps, not the territory itself, which always seemed rather odd to me.

Surely there is room for both—direct spiritual experience, and more accurate maps and models of those experiences. And surely both are crucially important in any Theory of Everything. Let us see.

THE RELATION OF SCIENCE AND RELIGION

Numerous theorists have classified the typical stances that have been taken concerning the relation of science and religion. All of these classifying schemes are basically quite similar, moving from warfare between science and religion, to peaceful coexistence, to mutual influence and exchange, to attempted integration.

Ian Barbour, for example, gives: (1) Conflict: science and religion are at war with each other; one is right and the other wrong, and that is that. (2) Independence: both can be "true," but their truths refer to basically separate realms, between which there is little contact. (3) Dialogue: science and religion can both benefit from a mutual dialogue, where the separate truths of each can mutually enrich the other. (4) Integration: science and religion are both part of a "big picture" that fully integrates their respective contributions.[2]

Eugenie Scott gives: (1) Warfare: science trumps religion, or religion trumps science; death to the loser. (2) Separate realms: science deals with natural facts, religion deals with spiritual issues; they neither conflict nor accord. (3) Accommodation: religion accommodates to the facts of science, using science to reinterpret, but not abandon, its core theological beliefs; a one-way street. (4) Engagement: both science and religion accommodate to each other, interacting as equal partners; a two-way street.[3]

In *The Marriage of Sense and Soul*, I give my own classification of the most common stances; here is a brief summary:

1. *Science denies religion.* This is still one of the most common stances among today's scientists, aggressively represented by such thinkers as Richard Dawkins, Francis Crick, and Steven Pinker. Religion is, pure and simple, either a superstitious relic

from the past, or, at best, a survival gimmick that nature uses to reproduce the species.

2. *Religion denies science.* The typical fundamentalist retort is that science is part of the fallen world and thus has no access to real truth. God created the world—and the entire fossil record—in six days, and that is that. The Bible is the literal truth, and so much the worse for science if it disagrees.

3. *Science and religion deal with different realms of being, and thus can peacefully coexist.* This is one of the most sophisticated stances, and it has two versions, strong and weak:

Strong version: *epistemological pluralism*—which maintains that reality consists of various dimensions or realms (such as matter, body, mind, soul, and spirit), and that science is dealing mostly with the lower realms of matter and body, while religion is dealing mostly with the higher realms of soul and spirit. In any event, both science and religion are equally part of a "big picture" that makes ample room for both, and their respective contributions can be integrated into this big picture. The traditional Great Chain of Being falls into this category (see fig. 4-3, p. 69). Representatives of something like this general view include Plotinus, Kant, Schelling, Coomaraswamy, Whitehead, Frithjof Schuon, Huston Smith, and Ian Barbour.

Weak version: *NOMA* ("nonoverlapping magisteria")— which is Stephen Jay Gould's term for the idea that science and religion are dealing with different realms, but these realms cannot be integrated into any sort of big picture since they are fundamentally incommensurate. They are both to be fully honored, but they cannot be fully integrated. By default, this is a very common stance among many scientists, who profess belief in some sort of Spirit, but cannot imagine how that would actually fit with science, so they render unto Caesar what is Caesar's, and render unto God what is left over.

4. *Science itself offers arguments for Spirit's existence.* This stance claims that many scientific facts and discoveries point directly to spiritual realities, and thus science can help us directly reveal God/dess. For example, the Big Bang seems to require some sort of Creator principle; evolution appears to be following an intelligent design; the anthropic principle implies that some

sort of creative intelligence is behind cosmic evolution, and so on. This is similar to Scott's one-way street accommodation, where science is used to enrich religion, but usually not vice versa. It is also similar to what Barbour calls "natural theology" as opposed to "a theology of nature" (in the former, Spirit is found directly from a reading of nature, as with many ecophilosophers; in the latter, a revealed Spirit is used to interpret nature in spiritual terms. Barbour favors the latter, which is part of category 3). This is a very common approach to this topic, and probably *the* most common among popular writers on the "new scientific paradigm which proves or supports mysticism."

5. *Science itself is not knowledge of the world but merely one interpretation of the world, and thus it has the same validity— no more, no less—as art and poetry.* This is, of course, the typical "postmodern" stance. Whereas the previous approach is the most common among popular writers on the topic of science and religion, this approach is the most common among the academic and cultural elite, who are not dedicated to constructing any sort of integration, but in deconstructing anything of worth that anybody else has to say on the issue. There are some truly important issues raised by postmodernists, and I have attempted to strongly include those points in a more integral view.[4] But left to its own devices, postmodernism is something of a dead end (see *Boomeritis*).

Now, most theorists offer those kinds of classifications happy that they cover all the bases, a summary of all of that is available. I offered that classification as a summary of everything that has not worked. All of those lists—from Barbour's to mine—are basically lists of failures, not successes. More accurately, some of those approaches (especially 3, 4, and 5) have provided key ingredients for what might yet be a truly integrated view, but none of them have sufficiently included the core of religion that I feel must be fully brought to the integrative table, namely: direct spiritual experience. And where some theorists do at least acknowledge spiritual experience (such as Barbour),[5] they are usually silent as to the revolutions in cognitive science, brain science, and contemplative phenomenology, which taken together point to a much more spectacular integration of science and religion than has heretofore been suggested.

I have summarized this more integral view as "all-quadrant, all-level," and I will now briefly outline its major points as they apply to science and spirituality.

NONOVERLAPPING MAGISTERIA?

Let us start with Stephen Jay Gould's approach—religion and science are both important, but belong to different and nonoverlapping realms—which is a view that a great number of both scientists and religionists maintain. Gould states, "The *lack of conflict* between science and religion [Gould is maintaining stance 3, weak version] arises from a *lack of overlap* between their respective domains of expertise—science in the empirical constitution of the universe, and religion in the search for proper ethical values and the spiritual meaning of our lives."[6] Gould acknowledges that, of course, science and religion "bump up against each other" all the time, and that friction provides much interesting light, and often unpleasant heat. But ultimately there is neither conflict nor accord between them, because they are apples and oranges.

In order to maintain this view, Gould has to create a rather rigid dualism between nature and human: "nature" will be the realm of facts (disclosed by science), and "human" will be the realm of values and meaning (disclosed by religion). "Nature can be truly 'cruel' and 'indifferent' in the utterly inappropriate terms of our ethical discourse—because nature does not exist for us, didn't know we were coming, and doesn't give a damn about us (speaking metaphorically)." Apparently, for Gould, humans are not fully part of nature; if we were, then human would simply be something that nature is doing. But nature doesn't give a damn about us, because "us" (or the part of us that engages in religion/ethics) and "nature" (of brute fact and no values) are two *nonoverlapping* realms. "I regard such a position as liberating, not depressing, because we then gain the capacity to conduct moral discourse—and nothing could be more important—in our *own terms*, free from . . . nature's factuality."[7]

It is this awkward dualism in any of its many forms—facts and values, nature and human, science and religion, empirical and spiritual, exterior and interior, objective and subjective—that has driven the attempts to find some sort of bigger picture that seamlessly weaves together these two realms, and does not simply proclaim them to be forever fated to work different sides of the street.

It is an intensely difficult and intricate problem. The standard theological response to the dualism "empirical versus spiritual" is to claim that Spirit created the empirical world, and thus they are related in that sense. If we can accord with God (and avoid evil), then we will be saved; if we deviate from God (and commit evil), we will be damned. But then the equally standard problem: if God created the world, and the world contains evil, then didn't God create evil? If so, then isn't God responsible for evil? So why blame me? If the product is broken, the fault lies with the manufacturer. (It appears that the relation of empirical and spiritual is not so easy to solve, after all.)

The eco-spirituality theorists fare no better. Instead of a transcendent, otherworldly God who creates nature, they postulate a purely immanent, this-worldly God/dess, namely, nature and nature's evolutionary unfolding. If we can accord with nature, we will be saved; if we deviate from nature, we will be doomed. But then the same problem: if nature (via evolution) produced humans, and humans produced the ozone hole, then didn't nature produce the ozone hole? If not, then there is some part of humans that is *not* part of nature, and therefore nature cannot be the ultimate ground of existence. Nature cannot be a genuine God or Goddess or Spirit—because nature is clearly *not* all-inclusive and thus must simply be a smaller slice of a much bigger pie. If so, what exactly is that Big Pie? And how, once again, do we actually heal this dualism between nature and human?

Many traditional theorists—from Plotinus to Huston Smith to Seyyed Nasr—attempt to handle these difficulties by resorting to the Great Chain of Being (a stance that is category 3, strong version). The idea is that there really aren't just two rigidly separate realms (such as matter and spirit), but at least four or five realms, infinitely shading into each other (such as matter, body, mind, soul, and spirit). The uppermost realm is the nondual ground of all the other realms, so that ultimate spirit suffers no final dualisms. However, as spirit steps down into creation, it gives rise to various dualisms that, although unavoidable in the manifest realm, can be healed and wholed in the ultimate or nondual realization of spirit itself.

Of all of the typical stances on the relation of science and religion, I have the most sympathy with that one (the traditional Great Chain), as I make clear in *The Marriage of Sense and Soul*. However, as I also point out in that book, the traditional presentation of the

Great Chain suffers a series of grave limitations, many of which are no different from those faced by the simpler dualistic models, such as Gould's.[8] For the traditionalists in effect postulate *four or five* nonoverlapping magisteria instead of just two, and even though those multiple magisteria (the many levels in the Great Chain) are often viewed as enveloping nests, the question still remains: what exactly is the relation of the higher realms, such as the spiritual, with the lower, such as the material?—and specifically in this sense: is science really confined exclusively to the lower realms (matter and body), and thus has little or nothing to tell us about the higher realms themselves (soul and spirit)? Is the relation between science and religion really that of a five-floor building, where science tells us all about the lower two floors, and religion tells us all about the higher two floors? The most respected responses in this debate—from Huston Smith to Ian Barbour to Stephen Jay Gould—are all variations on that theme (category 3, strong or weak).

But what if, instead of science telling us about one floor and religion about another, they both told us something different about each and every floor? What if science and religion were related, not as floors in a building, but as equal columns in a mansion? Not one on top of the other, but each alongside the other, all the way up and down? What then?

Well, if nothing else, this is an approach that has not yet been tried. Since the others have been found wanting, this might be worth investigating.

The Brain of a Mystic

Start with a simple example. A meditator is hooked to an EEG machine. As the meditator enters a deep contemplative state, the EEG machine shows an unmistakably novel series of brain wave patterns (such as the production of delta waves, which usually occur only in deep dreamless sleep). Moreover, the meditator claims that, in her direct experience of this delta state, she is having experiences for which the word "spiritual" seems most fitting: she is experiencing a sense of expanded consciousness, an increase in love and compassion, a feeling of encountering the sacred and numinous in both herself and the world at large. Other accomplished meditators who enter this state show the same objective set of brain wave patterns and report similar subjective states of spiritual experiences. What are we to make of this?

There is already a substantial body of research indicating that something like the above scenario happens quite often.[9] Let us simply assume, for the sake of argument, that the scenario is generally true. First of all, this shows immediately that the realms of science and religion, often thought to be "nonoverlapping magisteria," are in fact overlapping like crazy.

What the standard NOMA argument (category 3, in both its strong and weak form) tends to overlook is that, even if values and facts are in some sense separate realms, when a person experiences subjective values, those values have objective factual correlates in the brain itself. This is absolutely not to say that values can be reduced to brain states, or that spiritual experiences can be reduced to natural occasions. It is to say that spiritual realities (the magisteria of religion) and empirical realities (the magisteria of science) are not as compartmentalized as the typical solutions to this debate imagine.

An integral model—namely, all-quadrant, all-level—attempts to provide a framework in which all of those "facts," if you will, can be accommodated. The facts, that is, of both interior realities and exterior realities, "spiritual" experiences and "scientific" experiences, subjective realities and objective realities. It finds ample room for the traditional Great Chain of Being and Knowing—from matter to body to mind to soul to spirit—but it plugs those realities into empirical facts in a definite and specifiable fashion.

ALL-QUADRANT, ALL-LEVEL

As a preview, let's use a few simple diagrams to outline this integral approach of including both modern science and traditional religion in a possible Theory of Everything.

Figure 4-1 is the traditional Great Chain of Being, body to mind to soul to spirit. It is essentially similar to figures 3-3 and 3-4 (pp. 46 and 47). Because each senior level transcends but includes its juniors, this is actually the Great Nest of Being, as the figure suggests. In fact, the Great Chain of Being is the Great Holarchy of Being. This figure of the Great Nest is from Huston Smith's *Forgotten Truth: The Common Vision of the World's Religions*. Huston Smith is arguably the greatest living authority on the world's religions, and *Forgotten*

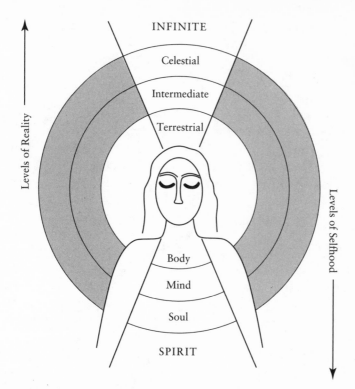

Figure 4-1. The Great Nest of Being. Adapted by permission from Huston Smith, Forgotten Truth: The Common Vision of the World's Religions *(San Francisco: HarperSanFrancisco, 1992, p. 62)*

Truth is his summary of the essential similarities shared by the world's great wisdom traditions. Figure 4-1 is a simple statement of the fact that every one of the great religious systems recognizes some version of body, mind, soul, and spirit. *It is a wonderfully simple summary of the traditional religious worldview found virtually the world over.* Figure 4-2, also prepared under the guidance of Smith, gives several examples of this.

Figures 4-1 and 4-2 both give only four levels, but most traditions have richer and more detailed maps as well. Some traditions give five levels; some give seven (as with the seven chakras [see chap. 6]); some give dozens. In figure 3-2 (p. 45), I gave a map with eleven levels (eight from Spiral Dynamics plus three higher ones). The exact number is less important than the fact that reality is understood to consist of several levels or waves of being and knowing.

In figure 4-3, I have presented a simple schematic of the Great

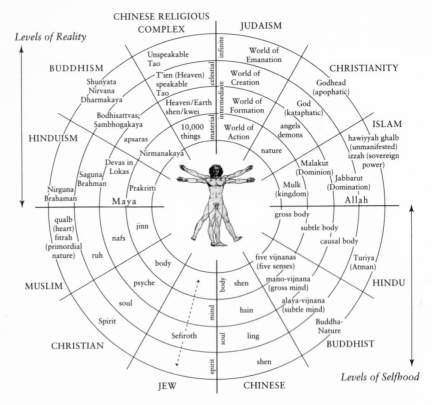

Figure 4-2. The Great Nest in Various Traditions.
Graphic layout courtesy of Brad Reynolds.

Nest emphasizing that it is a Great Holarchy. Notice that, *according to this traditional view*, science (e.g., physics, biology, psychology) is indeed on the lower floors, and religion (theology, mysticism) is on the top floors. (This is the basis for category 3, which, as we saw, is probably the most influential stance among those sympathetic with spirituality.) But this also gave the traditional Great Chain its "otherworldly" ontology; much of the upper floors were literally "out of this world" and had few if any points of contact with the material realm. (More specifically, the class of events marked D and E had virtually no direct correlations with A and B; hence, "otherworldly.")

The rise of modern science issued several lethal blows to that traditional conception. For example, modern research clearly demonstrated that consciousness (e.g., mind), far from being merely transcendental noumenon, was in fact anchored in many ways in the

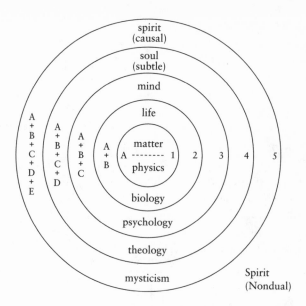

Figure 4-3. The Great Holarchy. Spirit is both the highest level (causal) and the nondual Ground of all levels.

organic, material brain—so much so that many modern scientists simply reduce consciousness to nothing but a play of neuronal systems. But we needn't follow scientific materialism to realize that consciousness is far from the disembodied essence imagined by most religious traditions. At the very least consciousness is intimately correlated with the biomaterial brain and the empirical organism, so that, whatever else their relation, science and religion are not simply "nonoverlapping magisteria."

The rise of modern science (particularly in the eighteenth century) was actually part of a whole series of events that have been described as "modernity." But they can all be summarized using Max Weber's idea of the "differentiation of the cultural value spheres" (the "values spheres" refer essentially to art, morals, and science). Where most premodern cultures failed to differentiate these spheres very clearly on a large scale, modernity differentiated art, morals, and science and let each pursue its own truths, in its own way, free from intrusion or violation from the others. (For example, in premodern Europe, Galileo could not look through his telescope and freely report what he saw, because science and church dogma were not yet separated. Modernity differentiated these spheres and set each free to follow its own course.) This resulted in the spectacular growth of scientific knowledge, a flurry of new approaches to art, and a sustained look at morals conceived in a more naturalistic light—resulted, that is, in many of the things that we now call "modern."

These "Big Three" spheres (art, morals, and science) basically refer to the realms of I, we, and it. Art refers to the aesthetic/expressive realm, the subjective realm described in first-person or "I" language. Morals refers to the ethical/normative realm, the intersubjective realm described in second-person or "we" language. And science refers to the exterior/empirical realm, the objective realm described in third-person or "it" language (which can actually be divided into two realms—the individual "it" and the collective "its"). This gives us four major realms: I, we, it, and its. Examples of each are given in figure 4-4 (whose terminology—none of which needs

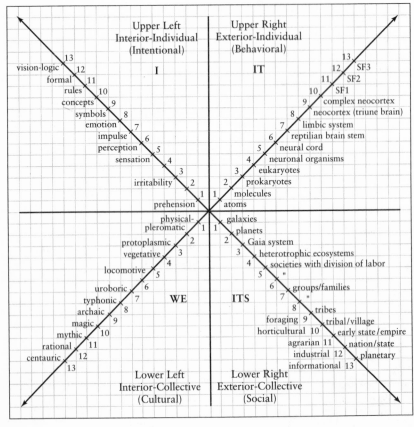

Figure 4-4. The Four Quadrants

to be learned!—is detailed in an endnote).[10] Again, all of this rather dry and abstract outline will be illustrated with concrete examples in the following pages.

In figure 4-4, notice that the two upper quadrants are singular or individual, and the two lower quadrants are plural or collective. The two left-hand quadrants are interior or subjective, and the two right-hand quadrants are exterior or objective.

The overall idea is fairly simple. Take, for example, the complex neocortex of the human being (10 on fig. 4-4). It can be described in *exterior*, objective, scientific terms (a series of material fissures in the outer layer of the brain consisting of various neuronal tissues, neurotransmitters, and organic pathways)—and that's the Upper Right. But when humans first evolved a complex neocortex, which separated them from the great apes, they moved from an *interior* meme of beige to an interior meme of purple (magic)—that is, there was a change, not just in *objective* brain structure, but also in the *subjective consciousness* from beige to purple, as the old archaic worldview gave rise to the magical worldview. These *interior* changes in the individual (the Upper Left) and in the collective (the Lower Left) are also shown in the figure. Finally, the collective group of early humans, when described in its *exterior* (material or social) forms,

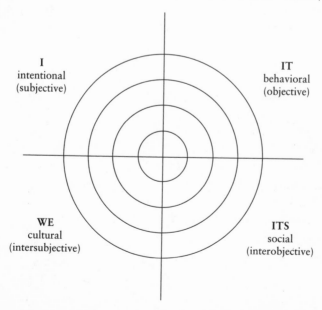

Figure 4-5. The Great Nest with the Four Quadrants

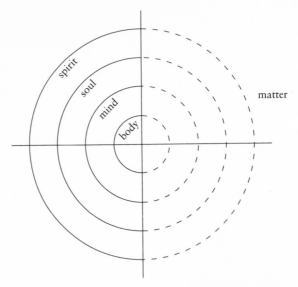

Figure 4-6. Correlations of Interior (Consciousness) with Exterior (Material) States

went from a beige survival band to an ethnic tribe (as shown in both figs. 3-1 and 4-4).

Now, all of those types of details (such as the structure of the neocortex, the scientific facts about various social systems, the cross-cultural memes of consciousness development, and so on), came to light largely with modern scientific investigation.

Figure 4-1, then, is a summary of the traditional, premodern, or "religious" worldview, and figure 4-4 is a summary of the modern, differentiated, or "scientific" worldview. For the moment, let's "integrate" them by simply superimposing one on the other. Of course, it is nowhere near that simple, and I have given extensive explanations of what this integration actually involves in several books.[11] But since this is a short introductory overview, let's just superimpose the modern conception on the premodern, as shown in figure 4-5. Also look at figure 4-6, which is figure 4-5 labeled to show the relation of the interior states (of *bodily* feeling, *mental* ideas, and *spiritual* experiences) with the exterior, *material* realms (investigated by objective science).

If the conception shown in figures 4-5 and 4-6 is valid, then we will have gone a long way toward integrating a premodern religious view with a modern scientific view. We would have integrated the

Great Nest of Being with the differentiations of modernity, one of the immediate gains of which would be a rather seamless integration of the religious and scientific realms and worldviews, in a way that would not violate the canons of either.

This integral approach would also satisfy the one criterion that we earlier said had not yet been tried, namely, that science (or exterior realities) and religion (or interior realities) would develop, not with one on top of the other (as in fig. 4-3), but with both *alongside* each other (as the Left- and Right-Hand aspects of an all-quadrant, all-level approach, as shown in figs. 4-5 and 4-6). Figure 4-6 can therefore easily explain the tricky scenario of the meditator hooked to the EEG machine. She is experiencing very real interior, subjective, spiritual realities (Upper-Left quadrant), but these also have very real exterior, objective, empirical correlates (Upper-Right quadrant), which the EEG machine dutifully registers. Science and religion are thus giving us some of the correlative facets—interior and exterior—of spiritual realities, and that is a key ingredient of their integration in a larger and more encompassing T.O.E.

GOOD SCIENCE

Wait just a minute, says the empirical scientist. I can follow the argument right up to the point that you give actual reality to the spiritual realms. Granted meditators are experiencing *something*, but it might be nothing more than a subjective emotional state. Who says it involves *actual realities*, in the same way that science deals with realities?

Here is where *The Marriage of Sense and Soul* takes a few more novel turns. To begin with, up to this point I have left "science" and "religion" (or "spirituality") undefined.[12] I have simply used those terms in the general way that most people use them. But in several books, I carefully outline the many different meanings that have been given to "science" and "religion" (*A Sociable God*, for example, outlines nine common but dramatically different meanings of "religion.") And much of this "science and religion" debate is a garbled mess because dozens of different definitions are being used without being identified.

In the area of spirituality, for instance, we need at the very least to distinguish between horizontal or *translative* spirituality (which seeks to give meaning and solace to the separate self and thus fortify the ego) and vertical or *transformative* spirituality (which seeks to transcend the separate self in a state of nondual unity consciousness that is beyond the ego). Let us simply call those "narrow religion" and "broad religion" (or shallow and deep, depending on your preferred metaphor).[13]

Likewise, with science, we need to distinguish between a narrow and a broad conception. Narrow science is based mostly on the exterior, physical, sensorimotor world. It is what we usually think of as the "hard sciences," such as physics, chemistry, and biology. But does this mean that science can tell us nothing about the interior domains at all? Surely there is a broader science that attempts to understand not just rocks and trees but humans and minds?

Well, in fact, we do acknowledge these types of broader sciences, sciences that are not rooted merely in the exterior, physical, sensorimotor world, but have something to do with interior states and qualitative research methodologies. We call these broader sciences the "human sciences" (the Germans call them the "geist" sciences, "geist" meaning mind or spirit). Psychology, sociology, anthropology, linguistics, semiotics, the cognitive sciences—all of these "broad sciences" attempt to use a generally "scientific" approach to the study of human consciousness. We have to be very careful that these approaches do not fall into merely aping the positivistic simplicity of the narrow sciences. But my point is that the difference between narrow science and broad science is already widely acknowledged. (We will return to this in a moment, but if you look at fig. 4-6, narrow sciences are those that study the Right-Hand or material quadrants, and broad sciences are those that attempt to study at least some aspects of the Left-Hand quadrants.)

The Marriage of Sense and Soul then proceeds to discuss just what it is that specifically defines broad religion and broad science. Start with broad science.

As we have already seen, we cannot define science—narrow or broad—by saying that it bases all of its knowledge on the sensorimotor world, because even narrow science (e.g., physics) uses a massive number of tools that are not empirical or sensorimotor, such as mathematics and logic. Mathematics and logic are *interior* realities (nobody has even seen the square root of negative one running around out there in the empirical world).

No, "science" is more a certain attitude of experimentation, honesty, and collaborative inquiry, and it grounds its knowledge, wherever it can, in *evidence* (whether that evidence is exterior, as in the narrow sciences, or interior, as in the broad sciences). The following three factors, I suggest, tend to define scientific inquiry in general, whether narrow or broad:

1. *A practical injunction or exemplar.* If you want to know whether it is raining or not, you must go to the window and look. The point is that "facts" are not lying around waiting for all and sundry to see. If you want to *know* this, you must *do* this—an experiment, an injunction, a pragmatic series of engagements, a social practice: these lie behind most forms of good science. This is actually the meaning of Kuhn's notion of "paradigm," which does not mean a super-theory but an exemplar or actual *practice.*

2. *An apprehension, illumination, or experience.* Once you perform the experiment or follow the injunction—once you pragmatically engage the world—then you will be introduced to a series of experiences or apprehensions that are *brought forth* by the injunction. These experiences are technically known as *data.* As William James pointed out, the real meaning of "datum" is *immediate experience.*[14] Thus, you can have physical experiences (or physical data), mental experiences (or mental data), and spiritual experiences (or spiritual data). All good science—whether narrow or broad—is anchored to some degree in data, or experiential evidence.

3. *Communal checking (either rejection or confirmation).* Once we engage the paradigm (or social practice) and bring forth a series of experiences and evidence (or data), it helps if we can check these experiences with others who have also completed the injunction and seen the evidence. A community of peers—or those who have adequately completed the first two strands (injunction and data)—is perhaps the best check possible, and all good science tends to turn to a community of the adequate for confirmation or rejection. This is where the principle of falsifiability is very useful. Although the fallibility criterion cannot stand on its own, as Sir Karl Popper believed, it is often an important ingredient in good science. The idea is simply that bad

data can be rejected by a community of the adequate. If there is no way that your belief system can be *challenged*, then there is no way to dislodge it at all, even if it is patently incorrect—and therefore whatever else you have, your beliefs are not very scientific (they are instead what is called "dogma," or a truth-claim backed only by authoritative fiat). Of course, there are many realities that are *not* open to the fallibility test—for example, you cannot reject, or even doubt, your own consciousness, as Descartes knew. But this third criteria simply says that good science constantly attempts to confirm (or reject) its knowledge claims, and the fallibility criterion is often used as one part of this third strand of good science.

DEEP RELIGION

Those three criteria are general characteristics of good science, whether narrow or broad. More specifically, they are characteristics of the way that good science, in any domain (physical, mental, spiritual), attempts to gather data and check its validity. Most forms of science also advance hypotheses to account for the data, and these hypotheses are then checked by a further application of the three strands of good science (further experiments, more data, see if they confirm or reject the hypothesis). In short, narrow science (whose data come mostly from the exterior realms or Right-Hand quadrants) and broad science (whose data come mostly from the interior realms or Left-Hand quadrants) *both attempt to be good science* (or science that follows the three strands of evidence accumulation and verification).

Let us then look briefly at religion. We have already seen that, as with science, there is a narrow religion (which seeks to fortify the separate self) and a broad or deep religion (which seeks to transcend the self). But what exactly is deep religion or *deep spirituality*, and how can it be *verified*? The claim, after all, is that in some sense deep spirituality is disclosing TRUTHS about the Kosmos, and is not merely a series of subjective emotional states. And here *The Marriage of Sense and Soul* makes a radical claim: Deep spirituality involves in part a *broad science of the higher levels of human development.*

THE INTEGRAL REVELATION

That is not the whole story of deep spirituality (as I will explain), but it is a crucial part of the story, a part that has not yet received sufficient attention. If you look at figure 4-3, which is the traditional Great Chain of Being, notice that there is a general unfolding from matter to body to mind to soul to spirit. These were traditionally (in Plotinus, for example) held to be both ontological levels of being and chronological levels of individual development. If you look at figure 4-4, you will see that the individual levels of development stop at vision-logic and the centaur (yellow/turquoise). The reason figure 4-4 does not contain the higher, transpersonal, supramental waves of consciousness (such as soul and spirit) is that this figure simply represents *average* evolution up to the present, and thus it does not show the higher waves of superconscious unfolding (although individuals can develop into these higher waves on their own). The claim of the great wisdom traditions is that there are indeed *higher stages* of consciousness development, so that we have available to us not just matter and body and mind, but also soul and spirit. I have indicated these higher waves in both figures 4-5 and 4-6 (as well as in the earlier fig. 3-2, pg. 45, although that was just for the Upper-Left quadrant—the point being that all these levels have correlates in all four quadrants).

My thesis is simply this: deep spirituality involves the *direct investigation of the experiential evidence disclosed in the higher stages of consciousness development*. (I have called these stages psychic, subtle, causal, and nondual—which are simply summarized as "soul" and "spirit" in the figures). These deep-spiritual investigations follow the three strands of all good science (not narrow science, good science). They rely on specific social *practices* or injunctions (such as contemplation); they rest their claims on data and *experiential* evidence; and they constantly refine and *check* these data in a community of the adequate—which is why they are correctly referred to as *contemplative sciences* (which is certainly how they understand themselves).

Thus, with reference to fig. 4-3, deep spirituality is, in part, the broad science of those phenomena, data, and experiences labeled D and E. (In fig. 4-6, D is labeled soul and E is labeled spirit.) But notice—and here is part of the novel claim of this approach—the interior data and experiences of soul and spirit (in the Upper-Left quadrant) *have correlates in the sensorimotor evidence in the Upper-Right quadrant* (see fig. 4-6). In other words, the deep spirituality of the Upper Left, which is investigated by broad science, has correlates in the Upper Right, which is investigated by narrow science. The contemplative and phenomenological sciences (the broad sciences of the interiors) can thus join hands with *good science* for direct experiential data in the Upper Left and with *narrow science* for correlative data in the Upper Right. (I repeat, the scientific aspects—both broad and narrow—of the higher realms are *not* the whole story, but they are a crucial part of the story that has constantly been overlooked; and they are certainly an important ingredient of any truly integral approach to this topic.)[15]

Thus, an "all-quadrant, all-level" approach intimately integrates science and religion across many different fronts. It integrates deep religion with broad science by showing that deep spirituality is in part a broad science of the farther reaches of human potential. It also integrates deep religion with narrow science, because even deep-spiritual data and experiences (such as mystical experiences) nonetheless have real correlates in the material brain, which can be carefully investigated with narrow science (as in the case of our meditator hooked to an EEG). It even makes room for narrow religion, as we will see in a moment. In all of these cases, an all-quadrant, all-level approach offers at least the possibility of a seamless intermeshing of what were previously though to be nonoverlapping magisteria.

Vive la Différence!

This integral approach also respects the *vital differences* between the various types of science and religion. To say that an inquiry is following the disposition of good science is not to say what the *content* or *actual methodology* of that inquiry will be. It only says that this inquiry engages the world (injunction), which brings forth experiences of the world (data), which are then checked as carefully as possible (confirmation). But the actual form of the inquiry—its methods and its content—will vary dramatically from level to level and from quadrant to quadrant. Unlike positivism, which allows only one method (empirical) in only one realm (sensorimotor), this approach allows as many methods and inquiries as there are levels and quadrants.

Thus, to give a very simple version, the phenomena labeled A, B, C, D, and E are all quite different entities, and methodologies have developed that deal with each of them in their own terms. In *Eye to Eye* I gave several reasons why none of these types of inquiries could be reduced to the others (I distinguished between sensorimotor experience, empiric-analytic, hermeneutic/phenomenological, mandalic, and gnostic). To the extent that any of those inquiries attempt to use injunctions (or pragmatic engagements), rest their claims in experiential evidence, and try to verify their claims as carefully as possible, then they can be called "good science." But beyond that, they differ dramatically, and those differences are fully honored—and even championed—in this integral approach.

Narrow Religion

The critical response to *Sense and Soul* was positive, with one major exception. By far the most common criticism (and the only serious criticism) was that by downplaying and often ignoring narrow religion, I was asking altogether too much from the religious side of the marriage. The average believer, the critics said, would never give up the myths and stories that constitute perhaps 95 percent of most forms of spirituality. Not only did the professional critics hammer this point, so did most of my friends who tried giving the book to, say, their parents, only to have their parents shake their heads: "What, no resurrection of Jesus? No Moses and the covenant? No facing Mecca each day in prayer? This isn't my religion." And so on.

Well, guilty. There is no doubt that I focused almost entirely on deep spiritual experiences (of the psychic, subtle, causal, and nondual realms), and ignored the much more common religious dimension of translative spirituality (or narrow religion). In all fairness, I did not deny that dimension or even suggest that it should be rejected. From *Sense and Soul*: "At the same time, this does not mean that we will lose all religious differences and local color, and fall into a uniform mush of homogenized . . . spirituality. The Great Chain is simply the skeleton of any individual's approach to the Divine, and on that skeleton each individual, and each religion, will bring appropriate flesh and bones and guts and glory. Most religions will continue to offer sacraments, solace, and myths (and other translative or horizontal consolations), in addition to the genuinely transformative practices of vertical contemplation. None of that necessarily needs to change dramatically for any religion. . . ."[16]

I did make two charges, however, which I still believe are true. One, if narrow religion makes *empirical* claims (i.e., claims about entities in the Right-Hand quadrants), then those claims must be put to the test of empirical (narrow) science. If religion claims that the earth was created in six days, let us test that empirical claim with empirical science. Most of those types of religious claims have spectacularly failed the test; you are free to believe them, but they cannot claim the sanction of either good science or deep spirituality. Two, the real core of religion is deep religion or deep spirituality, which tends to relax and lessen narrow-religion zeal, and thus, to the extent you are alive to your own higher potentials, you will find narrow religion less and less appealing.[17]

Of course, the critics are right that most people embrace a translative or narrow religion—whether belief in the Bible, or belief in Gaia, or belief in holistic systems theory—and do not wish to radically transform the *subject* of those beliefs. In my model, those types of mental beliefs refer to the magic, mythic, rational, or vision-logic levels of development (i.e., purple to turquoise). But I also wanted to address the higher or transpersonal realms (psychic, subtle, causal) beyond those mere beliefs—the superconscious and supramental realms that constitute the core of deep spirituality and the contemplative sciences. An "all-quadrant, all-level" model makes room for all of those occasions, from premental to mental to supramental.

SPIRITUALITY AND LIBERALISM

The last point I would like to discuss briefly on this topic is simple: Religion and science will never get along until religion and liberalism kiss and make up.

The classic Western Enlightenment—with its philosophy of *liberalism*—came into existence, in large measure, as an anti-religion movement. The liberal philosophers and political theorists of the Enlightenment sought, among other things, to liberate individuals from the dictates of state religion and the herd mentality, where, if you vocally disagreed with the Pope, the Spanish Inquisition had some interesting discussions with you. Liberalism maintained, on the contrary, that *the state should not promote any particular version of the good life*, but rather should let individuals decide for themselves (the separation of church and state). To this day, liberalism tends to be extremely suspicious of religion, simply because many religious believers do try to impose their values on others. Moreover, liberalism was also closely allied with the newly emerging natural sciences, from physics to biology to chemistry, which found little evidence for mythic religious beliefs (such as the universe being created in six days). For its part, mythic religion found liberalism to be not much more than a "ghastly and Godless atheism" that would ruin society. In short, liberalism and religion, almost from the start, tended to be deeply antagonistic toward each other.

But now that we have seen that are at least two different types of religion (narrow and deep), let us reframe this ancient animosity. The traditional religion that the Enlightenment questioned was blue religion, with its ethnocentric myths and absolutisms (believe in its mythic God, and you are saved; all disbelievers are eternally damned). The Enlightenment was instead representing the newly emerging, worldcentric, orange wave of existence, with its strong belief in scientific materialism, unilinear progress, commerce, and empiricism. The result was a titanic clash of memes, which eventually unleashed at least two revolutions (American and French).

The orange wave, we have seen, is the first truly postconventional and worldcentric wave of awareness. And thus, in many ways, the *philosophes* were indeed right to champion this rather extraordinary wave, with its emphasis on the universal rights of man (universal rights that, by their own logic, were soon extended to women, slaves, children, and even animals). This was a profound move from ethnocentric to worldcentric, from dominator social hierarchies toward meritocracies, from duty to dignity. And the philosophes were also quite right that most of the dogma of the mythic-membership religions were in fact superstitions with little evidence or proof. But they were deeply confused when they thought that *all* of traditional religion was nothing but Santa Claus myths. For every major wisdom tradition contains, at its core, a series of contemplative practices, and, at their best, these contemplative practices disclose the transrational and transpersonal waves of consciousness.[18] These contemplative sciences disclose, not *pre*rational myths, but *trans*rational realities, and the rational Enlightenment, alas, in reacting to all *non*-rational claims, carelessly threw both transrational and prerational out the window, and one enormously precious baby was tossed with tons of unpleasant bathwater.

Thus, with the Enlightenment, narrow scientific materialism (orange) took up a brutally adversarial stance toward almost all forms of religion (pre and trans).[19] To this day, religion tends to be identified with blue mythic-membership beliefs (belief in the literal truth of the Bible, the Torah, the Koran, etc.) and science tends to be identified with an intensely antireligious stance. My point is that *both* of them need to relax their narrow, shallow zealotry and open themselves to the good science and the deep spirituality of the higher waves of existence, where they both can find a deepening accord.

This would be a postconservative, postliberal spirituality. It would build on the gains of the worldcentric Enlightenment, and not retreat to merely mythic-membership pronouncements and prescriptive morality. That is to say, this is a spirituality that is not preliberal and reactionary, but progressive and evolutionary.[20] It does not seek to impose its belief structures on others, but invites each and all to develop their own potentials, therein to discover their own deep spirituality, radiant to infinity, glowing in the dark, happy for all time, this simple stunning discovery of your own Original Face, your divine soul and spirit, shining even now.

5

The RealWorld

We shall hang together, or we shall hang separately.
— BENJAMIN FRANKLIN

THE QUESTION I AM ASKED most often about this work is, What are its applications? That is, what are the applications of an integral or holonic model in the "real world"? What good is a T.O.E. even if we had one? Here is a brief sampling of what is going on.

INTEGRAL POLITICS

I have been working with Drexel Sprecher, Lawrence Chickering, Don Beck, Jack Crittenden, and several others toward an all-quadrant, all-level political theory (in addition to working with the writings of political theorists too numerous to list). We have been involved with advisors to Bill Clinton, Al Gore, Tony Blair, George W. Bush, and Jeb Bush, among others. There is a surprisingly strong desire, around the world, to find a more balanced and comprehensive politics that unites the best of liberal and conservative— President Clinton's *Vital Center*, George W. Bush's *Compassionate Conservatism*, Gerhard Schroeder's *Neue Mitte*, Tony Blair's *Third Way*, and Thabo Mbeki's *African Renaissance*, to name a few—and many theorists are finding an all-quadrant, all-level framework to be the sturdiest foundation for such.

Here is what I consider to be my own particular theoretical orientation, developed largely on my own, which has then become a framework for discussions with these other theorists, who bring their own original ideas for cross-fertilization. I will first indicate my own thoughts, and then the areas where these other theorists have helped me enormously.

In the last chapter of *Up from Eden* ("Republicans, Democrats, and Mystics"), I made the observation that, when it comes to the cause of human suffering, liberals tend to believe in exterior causes, whereas conservatives tend to believe in interior causes. That is, if an individual is suffering, the typical liberal tends to blame external social institutions (if you are poor it is because you are oppressed by society), whereas the typical conservative tends to blame internal factors (you are poor because you are lazy). Thus, the liberal recommends exterior social interventions: redistribute the wealth, change social institutions so that they produce fairer outcomes, evenly slice the economic pie, aim for equality among all. The typical conservative recommends that we instill family values, demand that individuals assume more responsibility for themselves, tighten up slack moral standards (often by embracing traditional religious values), encourage a work ethic, reward achievement, and so on.

In other words, the typical liberal believes mostly in Right-Hand causation, the typical conservative believes mostly in Left-Hand causation. (Don't let the terminology of the quadrants confuse you—the political Left believes in Right-Hand causation, the political Right believes in Left-Hand causation; had I been thinking of political theory when I arranged the quadrants, I would probably have aligned them to match.)

The important point is that the first step toward an *integral politics* that unites the best of liberal and conservative is to recognize that *both* the interior quadrants and the exterior quadrants are equally real and important. We consequently must address both interior factors (values, meaning, morals, the development of consciousness) and exterior factors (economic conditions, material well-being, technological advance, social safety net, environment)—in short, a truly integral politics would emphasize both interior development and exterior development.

Let us therefore focus for a moment on the area of interior consciousness development. This is, after all, the hardest part for liberals to accept, because the discussion of "stages" or "levels" of anything (including consciousness) is deeply antagonistic to most liberals, who believe that all such "judgments" are racist, sexist, marginalizing, and so on. The typical liberal, recall, does not believe in interior causation, or sometimes even in interiors for that matter. The typical liberal epistemology (e.g., John Locke) imagines that the mind is a tabula rasa, a blank slate, that is filled with pictures of the external world. If something is wrong with the interior (if you are suffering), it is because something is first wrong with the exterior (the social institutions)—because your interior comes from the exterior.

But what if the interior has its own stages of growth and development, and is not simply imported from the external world? If a genuinely integral politics depends upon including both interior development and exterior development, then it would behoove us to look carefully at these interior stages of consciousness unfolding. In books such as *Integral Psychology*, I have correlated over one hundred developmental models of consciousness, West and East, ancient and modern, which help to give us a very solid picture of the stages of development of the subjective realm—not as a rigid series of unalterable levels but as a general guide to the possible waves of consciousness unfolding.

If the first step toward an integral politics is to combine the interior and the exterior (the Left-Hand and the Right-Hand, the subjective and objective), the second step is to understand that there are *stages of the subjective*—stages, that is, of consciousness evolution. To help elucidate these stages, we can use any of the more reputable maps of interior development, such as those of Jane Loevinger, Robert Kegan, Clare Graves, William Torbert, Susanne Cook-Greuter, or Beck and Cowan's Spiral Dynamics. For this simplified overview, I will use just three broad stages: preconventional (or egocentric), conventional(orsociocentric), and postconventional (or worldcentric).

The traditional conservative ideology is rooted in a conventional, mythic-membership, sociocentric wave of development. Its values tend to be grounded in a mythic religious orientation (such as the Bible); it usually emphasizes family values and patriotism; it is strongly sociocentric (and therefore often ethnocentric); with roots as well in aristocratic and hierarchical social values (blue meme) and a tendency toward patriarchy and militarism. This type of mythic-membership and civic virtue dominated cultural consciousness from approximately 1,000 BCE to the Enlightenment in the West, whereupon a fundamentally new average mode of consciousness—

the rational-egoic (postconventional, worldcentric, orange meme)—emerged on an influential scale, bringing with it a new mode of political ideology, namely, liberalism.

The liberal Enlightenment understood itself to be in large measure a reaction against the mythic-membership structure and its fundamentalism, in two aspects especially: the socially oppressive power of myths with their ethnocentric prejudices (e.g., all Christians are saved, all heathens go to hell), and the nonscientific nature of the knowledge claimed by myths (e.g., the universe was created in six days). Both the active oppression instituted by mythic/ethnocentric religion and its nonscientific character were responsible for untold suffering, and the Enlightenment had as one of its goals the alleviation of this suffering. Voltaire's battle cry—which set the tone of the Enlightenment—was "Remember the cruelties!"—the suffering inflicted by the Church on millions of people in the name of a mythic God.

In place of an ethnocentric mythic-membership, based on a role identity in a hierarchy of other role identities, the Enlightenment sought an ego identity free from ethnocentric bias (the universal rights of man) and based on rational and scientific inquiry. Universal rights would fight slavery, democracy would fight monarchy, the autonomous ego would fight the herd mentality, and science would fight myth: this is how the Enlightenment understood itself (and in many cases, rightly so). In other words, *at its best* the liberal Enlightenment represented—and was a product of—the evolution of consciousness from conventional/sociocentric to postconventional/worldcentric.

Now had liberalism been just that—the product of an evolutionary advance from ethnocentric to worldcentric—it would have won the day, pure and simple. But, in fact, liberalism arose in a climate that I have called *flatland*. Flatland—or scientific materialism—is the belief that only matter is real, and that only *narrow science* has any claim to truth.[1] (Narrow science, recall, is the science of any Right-Hand domain, whether that be atomistic science of the Upper Right or systems science of the Lower Right.) Flatland, in other words, is the belief that only the Right-Hand quadrants are real.

And liberalism, arising directly in the midst of this scientific materialism, swallowed its worldview hook, line, and sinker. In other words, *liberalism became the political champion of flatland*. The

only thing that is ultimately real is the Right-Hand, material, sensorimotor world; the mind itself is just a tabula rasa, a blank slate
that is filled with representations of the Right-Hand world; if the
subjective realm is ill, it is because objective social institutions are ill;
the best way to free men and women is therefore to offer them mate-
rial-economic freedom; thus scientific materialism and economic
equality are the major routes of ending human suffering. *The interior realms*—the entire Left-Hand domains—are simply ignored or
even denied. All interiors are equal—no stance is better than another—and that ends that discussion.[2] There are no waves, stages, or
levels of consciousness, for that would be to make a ranking judgment, and ranking is very, very bad. A noble sentiment, but it gutted
the interiors altogether, and pledged allegiance to flatland.

Nonetheless, this desire to alleviate human suffering is applied
universally—all people are to be treated fairly, regardless of race,
color, sex, or creed (the move from ethnocentric to worldcentric).
Thus, liberal political theory was coming from a higher level of
development, but a development that was caught in pathological
flatland. Put bluntly, liberalism was a sick version of a higher level.

That is the great irony of liberalism. Theorists have long agreed
that traditional liberalism is inherently self-contradictory, because it
champions equality and freedom, and you can have one or the other
of those, not both. I would explain the root of this contradiction as
follows: Liberalism was itself the product of a whole series of interi-
or stages of consciousness development—from egocentric to ethnocentric to worldcentric—whereupon it turned around and denied the
importance or even the existence of those interior levels of development! Liberalism, in championing only exterior causation (i.e., flatland), denied the interior path that produced liberalism.[3] *The liberal
stance itself is the product of stages that it then denies*—and there is
the inherent contradiction of liberalism.

Liberalism thus refused to make any "judgments" about the
interiors of individuals—no stance is better than another!—and
instead focused merely on finding ways to fix the exterior, economic,
social institutions; and thus it completely abandoned the interiors
(values, meanings, interior development) to the conservatives.
The conservatives, on the other hand, fully embraced interior development—but only up to the mythic-membership stage, which is
nonetheless healthy as far as it goes: a healthy version of a lower
level. (Mythic-membership, civic virtue, the blue meme, the conven-

tional/conformist stage of development—this is a normal, healthy, natural, *necessary* wave of human development, and this sturdy social structure is still the main base of traditional conservative politics.)[4]

So here is the truly odd political choice that we are given today: a sick version of a higher level versus a healthy version of a lower level—liberalism versus conservatism.

The point is that a truly integral politics would embrace a *healthy* version of the *higher* level—namely, grounded in the postconventional/worldcentric waves of development, it would equally encourage *both* interior development and exterior development—the growth and development of consciousness and subjective well-being, as well as the growth and development of economic, social, and material well-being. It would be, in other words, an "all-quadrant, all-level" political theory and practice.[5]

Moreover, from this spacious vantage point, the prime directive of a genuine integral politics would be, not to try to get everybody to a particular level of consciousness (integral, pluralistic, liberal, or whatever), but to *ensure the health of the entire spiral of development* at all of its levels and waves. Thus the two steps toward an integral politics are: (1) including both interior and exterior, and (2) understanding stages of the interior and thus arriving at the prime directive.[6]

That is the general orientation that I have brought into the political discussions with the aforementioned theorists. From Chickering (*Beyond Left and Right*) and Sprecher I have adopted the important distinction between "order" and "free" wings within both conservatism and liberalism, referring to whether emphasis is placed on collective or individual ends.[7] They independently agree with my general definition of Left as believing in exterior causation and Right as believing in interior causation.[8] The order wings of both Left and Right wish to impose their beliefs on all, usually via government, whereas the free wings of both ideologies place the rights of individuals first. For example, those who wish the state to use its authority to reinforce conventional roles and values are order Right, while the politically correct movement and orthodox feminists who wish to use the state to enforce their version of equality are order Left. Free-market economic libertarians are generally free Right; civil libertarians are generally free Left.

Those political quadrants happen to align, in significant ways, with my four quadrants, because the upper quadrants are individual or "free," and the lower quadrants are collective or "order"; the interior quadrants are right/conservative, and the exterior quadrants are left/liberal.[9] This shows us which quadrant a particular theorist thinks is the most important (and therefore should be manipulated, addressed, or protected in attempting to achieve policy outcomes). The idea, of course, is that all four quadrants are unavoidably important in reality. Thus, an all-quadrant, all-level approach once again can serve as a theoretical basis for a truly integrated political orientation.

Jack Crittenden (*Beyond Individualism*) has been applying the notion of compound individuality developed in *Up from Eden* to political and educational theory, and has constantly added to my own understanding of these ideas. Don Beck's Spiral Dynamics (developed with Christopher Cowan) is a wonderful elucidation of Clare Graves's pioneering work, and has had numerous applications in the "real world," from politics to education to business, and I have benefited greatly from those many discussions as well. Beck probably has as good an understanding of the prime directive as anybody, and my own formulations have been enriched by his work. Jim Garrison, as president of the State of the World Forum, has had extensive experience about how an integral vision will—and often will not—play out on the world stage. Michael Lerner's "Politics of Meaning," though embedded in order-Left assumptions and thus not an integral approach, is nonetheless an uncommon and admirable attempt to get liberals to look at the interior quadrants (meaning, value, spirituality), which they have classically avoided like the plague, an avoidance that has had dire consequences (e.g., the interiors have been left to the conservatives and their often reactionary, mythic-membership values, which are fine as a partial foundation of society, disastrous when left exclusively to their own devices).

INTEGRAL GOVERNANCE

In all of this, we are looking for hints as to what a second-tier or *integral* approach to governance might look like.

The Constitution of the United States is generally a moral-stage 5 document (postconventional and worldcentric). At the time it was written, perhaps 10 percent of the U.S. population was actually at moral stage 5. The brilliance of this document is that it found a way to institutionalize the worldcentric, postconventional stance and let it act as a governance system for people who were not, for the most part, at that higher level. The Constitution itself thus became a *pacer of transformation*, gently encouraging every activity within its reach to stand within a worldcentric, postconventional, non-ethnocentric moral atmosphere. The brilliance of this document and its framers is hard to overstate.

The U.S. Constitution was the culmination of first-tier governance philosophy. Even though its framers were often using second-tier thinking, the realities that they were addressing were still almost entirely first-tier, particularly the formation and relation of the *corporate states* that evolved out of *feudal empires* and *ancient nations*.

But now *global systems* and *integral meshworks* are evolving out of corporate states and value communities (see fig. 3-1). These interdependent systems require governance capable of integrating (*not* dominating) nations and communities over the entire spiral of interior and exterior development. What the world now needs is the first genuinely second-tier form of political philosophy and governance. I believe, of course, that it will be an all-quadrant, all-level political theory and practice, deeply integral in its structures and patterns. This will in no way replace the U.S. Constitution (or that of any other nation), but will simply situate it in global meshworks that facilitate mutual unfolding and enhancement—an integral and holonic politics.

The question remains: exactly how will this be conceived, understood, embraced, and practiced? What precise details, what actual specifics, where and how and when? This is the great and exhilarating call of global politics at the millennium.[10] We are awaiting the new global founding Fathers and Mothers who will frame an integral system of governance that will call us to our more encompassing future, that will act as a gentle pacer of transformation for the entire spiral of human development, honoring each and every wave as it unfolds, yet kindly inviting each and all to even greater depth.

INTEGRAL MEDICINE

Nowhere are the four quadrants more immediately applicable than in medicine, and the model is being increasingly adopted by health-care facilities around the world. A quick trip through the quadrants will show why an integral model can be helpful. (In this example we are talking about physical illnesses—a broken bone, cancer, heart disease, etc.—and how best to treat them, since that is the focus of most orthodox medicine.)

Orthodox or conventional medicine is a classic Upper-Right quadrant approach. It deals almost entirely with the physical organism using physical interventions: surgery, drugs, medication, and behavioral modification. Orthodox medicine believes essentially in the physical causes of physical illness, and therefore prescribes mostly physical interventions. But the holonic model claims that every physical event (UR) has at least four dimensions (the quadrants), and thus even physical illness must be looked at from all four quadrants (not to mention levels, which we will address later). The integral model does not claim the Upper-Right quadrant is not important, only that it is, as it were, only one fourth of the story.

The recent explosion of interest in alternative care—including such disciplines as psychoneuroimmunology—has made it quite clear that the person's *interior states* (emotions, psychological attitude, imagery, and intentions) play a crucial role in both the *cause* and the *cure* of even physical illness. In other words, the Upper-Left quadrant is a key ingredient in any comprehensive medical care. Visualization, affirmation, and conscious use of imagery have been shown to play a significant role in the management of most illnesses, and outcomes have been shown to depend on emotional states and mental outlook.[11]

But as important as those subjective factors are, individual consciousness does not exist in a vacuum; it exists inextricably embedded in shared cultural values, beliefs, and worldviews. How a culture (LL) views a particular illness—with care and compassion or derision and scorn—can have a profound impact on how an individual copes (UL) with that illness, which can directly affect the course of the physical illness itself (UR). In fact, many illnesses cannot even be defined without reference to a shared cultural background (just like what you consider to be a "weed" often depends on what you are trying to grow in the first place). The Lower-Left quadrant includes all of the enormous number of *intersubjective* factors that are crucial in any human interaction—such as the shared communication between doctor and patient; the attitudes of family and friends and how they are conveyed to the patient; the cultural acceptance (or derogation) of the particular illness (e.g., AIDS); and the very values of the culture that the illness itself threatens. All of those factors are to some degree causative in any physical illness and cure (simply because *every* holon has four quadrants).

Of course, in practice, this quadrant needs to be limited to those factors that can be effectively engaged—perhaps doctor and patient communication skills, family and friends support groups, and a general understanding of cultural judgments and their effects on illness. Studies consistently show, for example, that cancer patients in support groups live longer than those without similar cultural support. Some of the more relevant factors from the Lower-Left quadrant are thus crucial in any comprehensive medical care.

The Lower-Right quadrant concerns all those material, economic, and social factors that are almost never counted as part of the disease entity, but in fact—like every other quadrant—are *causative* in both disease and cure. A social system that cannot deliver food will kill you (as famine-racked countries demonstrate daily, alas). But even in developed countries: If you have a lethal but treatable disease, and your insurance plan is the only source of funding you have, and your plan does not cover your disease, you will die. The cause of your death: poverty. Because we usually don't think like this, we say, "The virus killed him." The virus is part of the cause; the other three quadrants are just as much a cause. When the FDA was holding up drugs that might help AIDS, a gentleman with the disease stood before Congress and said, "Don't let my epitaph read, 'He died of red tape.'" But that is exactly right. In the real world, where every entity has all four quadrants, a virus in the UR quadrant might be the focal issue, but without a social system (LR) that can deliver treatment, you will die. That is not a separate issue; it is central to the issue, because all holons have four quadrants. The Lower-Right quadrant includes factors such as economics, insurance, social delivery systems, and even things as simple as how a hospital room is physically laid out (does it allow ease of movement, access to visitors, etc.)—not to mention items like environmental toxins.

The foregoing items refer to the "all-quadrant" aspect of the cause and cure (or management) of illness. The "all-level" part refers to the fact that individuals have—at least—physical, emotional, mental, and spiritual levels in each of those quadrants (see figs. 4-5 and 4-6). Some illnesses have largely physical causes and physical cures (get hit by a bus, break your leg, physically set and plaster it). But most illnesses have causes and cures that include *emotional, mental,* and *spiritual* waves. I have covered these specific levels in *Grace and Grit* and won't repeat myself here; and literally hundreds of researchers from around the world have added immeasurably to our understanding of the "multi-level" nature of disease and cure (including invaluable additions from the great wisdom traditions, shamanic to Tibetan). The point is simply that by adding these levels to the quadrants, a much more comprehensive—and effective—medical model begins to emerge.

In short, a truly effective and comprehensive medical plan would be all-quadrant, all-level: the idea is simply that each quadrant or dimension—I, we, and it—has physical, emotional, mental, and spiritual levels or waves (fig. 4-6), and a truly integral treatment would take all of these realities into account. Not only is this type of integral treatment more *effective*, it is for that reason more *cost-efficient*—which is why even organizational medicine is looking at it more closely. Of the hundreds of theorists doing wonderful work in this regard, I might mention John Astin, who has written perceptively on the application of holonic theory to complementary and alternative medicine[12]; Pat Odgen and Kekuni Minton[13]; Gary Schwartz and Linda Russek[14]; Wanda Jones and James Ensign (of New Century Healthcare Institute); and Barbara Dossey and Larry Dossey, who have used holonic theory to supplement their own extensive and original work in "the great chain of healing."[15]

A group of us have recently formed Integral Institute, with branches of integral medicine, integral psychology, integral politics, and so on (see below). Members of the Institute of Integral Medicine include, in addition to the theorists listed in the previous paragraph, Ken Pelletier, Mike Murphy, George Leonard, Marilyn Schlitz, Joan Borysenko, Jeanne Achterberg, and Jon Kabat-Zinn. Members of Integral Institute do not necessarily agree with all the details of my version of integralism, but they do share a deep interest in a more integral, balanced, comprehensive vision, spanning the spectrum from matter to mind to spirit, exercised in self and culture and nature.

INTEGRAL BUSINESS

Applications of the holonic model have recently exploded in business, perhaps, again, because the applications are so immediate and obvious. The quadrants give the four "environments" or dimensions in which a product must survive, and the levels give the types of values that will be both producing and buying the product. Research into the values hierarchy—such as Maslow's and Graves's (e.g., Spiral Dynamics), which has already had an enormous influence on business and "VALS"—can be combined with the quadrants (which show how these levels of values appear in the four different environments) to give a truly comprehensive map of the marketplace (which covers both traditional markets and cybermarkets). Of course, this can be used in a cynical and manipulative way—business, after all, is business—but it can also be used in an enlightened and efficient fashion to more fruitfully match human beings with needed products and services (thus promoting the health of the overall spiral).

Moreover, *management and leadership training* programs, based on an integral model, have also begun to flourish. Daryl Paulson, in "Management: A Multidimensional/Multilevel Perspective," shows that there are four major theories of business management (Theory X, which stresses individual behavior; Theory Y, which focuses on psychological understanding; cultural management, which stresses organizational culture; and systems management, which emphasizes the social system and its governance). Paulson then shows that these four management theories are in fact the four quadrants, and that an integral model would necessarily include all four approaches. He then moves to the "all-level" part, and suggests a simplified but very useful four stages that the quadrants go through, with specific suggestions for implementing a more "all-quadrant, all-level" management.[16]

Other pioneers in this area include Geoffrey Gioja and JMJ Associates, whose Integral Leadership seminars (which use three levels in the four quadrants) have been presented to dozens of *Fortune* 500 companies ("We believe that until recently, the transformational approach of organizational change has been the unmatched champion for producing breakthroughs, both subjective and objective.[17] We now assert that the transformational approach has been eclipsed by the integral approach."); John Forman of R.W. Beck Associates, who uses an all-quadrant, all-level approach to supplement (and correct the flatland distortions of) systems and complexity theory; On Purpose Associates (John Cleveland, Joann Neuroth, Pete Plastrik, Deb Plastrik); Bob Anderson, Jim Stuart, and Eric Klein (co-author of *Awakening Corporate Soul*), whose Leadership Circle brings an all-quadrant, all-level approach to "Integral Transformation and Leadership" ("The main point is that the evolution of all of these streams of development in all of the quadrants are intimately bound up with each other. Spiritual intelligence is literacy in the practice of transformation. Spiritual intelligence is fast becoming a leadership imperative."); Leo Burke, Director and Dean of Motorola's University College of Leadership and Transcultural Studies, who oversees the training of some 20,000 managers around the world; Ian Mitroff (*A Spiritual Audit of Corporate America*); Ron Cacioppe and Simon Albrecht ("Developing Leadership and Management Skills Using the Holonic Model and 360 Degree Feedback Process"); Don Beck of Spiral Dynamics, which has been used in situations totaling literally hundreds of thousands of people; and Jim Loehr and Tony Schwartz, who are working with an all-quadrant, all-level approach coupled with very specific change technologies built around the optimal management of energy—physical, emotional, and mental. Tony is now writes the monthly Life/Work column for *Fast Company* and can be contacted there. All of the above individuals have joined the Institute of Integral Business, along with Deepak Chopra, Joe Firmage (Project Voyager), Bob Richards (Clarus), Sam Bercholz (Shambhala), Fred Kofman, Bill Torbert, Warren Bennis, and numerous others.

INTEGRAL EDUCATION

Because I am an "integral" or "holistic" thinker, people often imagine that I support what are generally called "holistic" educational approaches, whether conventional or alternative. Alas, such is not generally the case. Many "holistic" approaches are, in my opinion, either sadly flatland (based on systems theory, or merely the Lower-Right quadrant), or they stem ponderously and rather exclusively from the green meme, which means a type of pluralistic approach that nobly attempts not to marginalize other approaches, but in fact marginalizes hierarchical development, and thus often ends up sabotaging actual growth and evolution. In any event, most of these typical holistic approaches overlook the prime directive, which is that it is the health of the overall spiral, and not any one level, that is the central ethical imperative. A truly integral education does not simply impose the green meme on everybody from day one, but rather understands that development unfolds in phase-specific waves of increasing inclusiveness. To use Gebser's version, consciousness fluidly flows from archaic to magic to mythic to rational to integral waves, and a genuinely integral education would emphasize, not just the last wave, but *all* of them as they appropriately unfold.

There are a large number of truly integral theorists working with these ideas and the applications of an all-quadrant, all-level education. In many instances, both the organizational structure of the schools (administration and faculty) and the core curriculum offered to students have been organized around an all-quadrant, all-level format. This has occurred both in conventional schools and in schools for the developmentally challenged. This overall topic is a prime focus of the Institute of Integral Education.

CONSCIOUSNESS STUDIES

The dominant approach to consciousness studies in this country is still that of narrow science (i.e., a cognitive science based largely on the Upper-Right quadrant). As I suggest in *Integral Psychology*, a more comprehensive approach to consciousness studies might start by using all four quadrants, or simply the Big Three of I, we, and it (first-person phenomenal accounts of consciousness; second-person intersubjective structures; and third-person scientific systems). This type of "1-2-3" of consciousness studies has already begun, as evidenced in such books as *The View From Within*, edited by Francisco Varela and Jonathan Shear, and by many articles carried regularly in *The Journal of Consciousness Studies*. The next stage of a more comprehensive approach might include not just "all-quadrant" but "all-level," and in *Integral Psychology* I outline ways in which that important next step might be implemented.

Several theorists who are interested in a more comprehensive and balanced approach to psychology and consciousness studies have formed the Institute of Integral Psychology. Its members include Roger Walsh, Frances Vaughan, Robert Kegan, Susanne Cook-Greuter,

Jenny Wade, Kaisa Puhakka, Don Beck, Robert Forman, Richard Mann, Brian van der Horst, Allan Combs, Raz Ingrasci, Antony Arcari, T George Harris, Francisco Varela, Connie Hilliard, and Michael Murphy, among others.

RELATIONAL AND SOCIALLY ENGAGED SPIRITUALITY

The major implication of an all-level, all-quadrant approach to spirituality is that physical, emotional, mental, and spiritual waves of being should be simultaneously exercised in self, culture, and nature (i.e., in the I, we, and it domains). There are many variations on this theme, ranging from integral transformative practice to socially engaged spirituality to relationships as spiritual path. The number of truly impressive groups and organizations pioneering these types of approaches is too large to list. But perhaps mention could be made of the work of Thich Nhat Hanh, Diana Winston, Donald Rothberg, *Tikkun* magazine, and Robert Forman and the Forge Institute (of which I am a member), who are attempting to bring some fresh perspectives to this noble endeavor.

INTEGRAL ECOLOGY

The approach to ecology set forth in *Sex, Ecology, Spirituality* is, critics agreed, a unique approach. Whether the critics liked the book or not, they agreed it was unique because it managed to combine ecological unity, systems theory, and nondual spirituality, but without privileging the biosphere and without using the Web-of-Life notion, which I maintain is a reductionistic, flatland conception. Rather, an all-quadrant, all-level approach to ecology allows us to situate the physiosphere, the biosphere, the noosphere, and the theosphere in their appropriate relationships in the Kosmos at large, and thus we can emphasize the crucial importance of the biosphere without having to *reduce* everything to the biosphere.

The key to these relationships—and the reason why they have so often been confused—can be seen in figure 4-6. Notice that the body (biosphere), mind (noosphere), and soul/spirit (theosphere) are all indicated on the figure. Each senior wave transcends and includes its junior, as shown by the enveloping nests. *In that sense*, it is quite correct to say that the mind transcends and includes the body, or that the noosphere transcends and includes the biosphere. The biosphere is a crucial component of the noosphere, but not vice versa (as most ecologists incorrectly suppose). That is, you can destroy the noosphere—or human minds—and the biosphere will still survive quite handsomely; but if you destroy the biosphere, all human minds are also destroyed. The reason is that the biosphere is a part of the noosphere, and not vice versa. By analogy, an atom is part of a molecule; if you destroy the molecule, the atom can still exist, but if you destroy the atom, the molecule is also destroyed. Same for biosphere and noosphere: destroy the latter, and the former can still exist, but not vice versa, showing that on the interior realms, the biosphere is a part of the noosphere, and not the other way around (as can be clearly seen in figs. 4-3 and 4-6). So it is *not* true that human minds (the noosphere) are part of nature (or the biosphere), but rather the reverse.

But notice, every interior event has a correlate in the exterior sensory world—the world we often call "nature." Thus, most ecotheorists look at the external, empirical, sensory world, and they conclude that "*Everything* is a part of nature," because everything does indeed have a correlate in the Right-Hand world (as can be seen in figs. 4-4 and 4-6). So they conclude that "nature" (or the "biosphere") is the ultimate reality, and they ask that we act in accord with "nature," and thus they reduce everything to some version of ecology or the biosphere or the great Web of Life. But that is only *half* the story, the Right-Hand half. On the *interior* or Left-Hand dimensions, we see that nature—or the sensory, felt, empirical dimensions—are only a small part of the bigger story, a small slice of the Bigger Pie, a Pie that includes biosphere, noosphere, and theosphere. And although all of those interior waves have exterior correlates in the world of nature, they cannot be reduced to those exteriors; *they cannot be reduced to nature.* To do so is simply to embrace yet another version of flatland: the monochrome world of Right-Hand reality, the empirical-sensory Web of Life. That is ecological reductionism at its worst—reducing the entire Kosmos to the Lower-Right quadrant—a reductionism at the heart of many ecophilosophies.

On the other hand, an all-quadrant, all-level approach to ecology—as summarized in figure 4-6—allows us to honor the physiosphere, the biosphere, the noosphere and theosphere, not by trying to reduce one to the others, but by acknowledging and respecting the vitally crucial role they all play in this extraordinary Kosmos.[18]

MINORITIES OUTREACH

Since a truly integral model does not try to take one level or dimension of development (such as pluralistic, transpersonal, or even integral) and try to force it on everybody, but instead follows the prime directive of working for the health of the overall spiral of development, its approach to minorities is considerably different from typical liberal, conservative, and countercultural approaches. What is required is *not* to force liberal pluralism, conservative values, green multiculturalism, or holistic ideas on anybody, but to foster the conditions—both interior and exterior—that will allow individuals and cultures to develop through the spiral at their own rate, in their own way.[19] The same is true for a more integral approach to developing countries. A specific example from UNICEF is worth examining.

ALL-QUADRANTS, ALL-LEVELS, ALL-LINES: AN OVERVIEW OF UNICEF

"The Process of Integral Development" and "The Integrative Approach: All-Quadrants, All-Levels, All-Lines" are two in a series of presentations by iSchaik Development Associates, consultants for UNICEF. They outline the four quadrants, with examples from each; they summarize the major levels or waves in each quadrant; and they signal the importance of the numerous developmental lines or streams progressing in a relatively independent manner through the various waves. (See fig. 5-1, which was prepared by iSchaik Development Associates.) They state that "This is the bigger picture within which all the ideas and developments with which UNICEF is involved must be seen."

They then move to specifics: "In order to deepen our understanding of the complex and interrelated nature of our world, a mapping of consciousness development in social and cultural evolution is crucial. This must also have an integral approach to ensure that evolu-

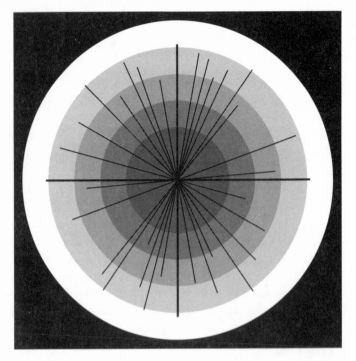

Figure 5-1. UNICEF (iSchaik Development Associates)

tion, and thus the state of children, humanity, culture and society, returns to a state of sustainable process." They point out that "this requires a framework that allows us to go deeper than the understanding of the mere objective/surface system or web, and wider than a cultural understanding of diversity." In other words, we must go beyond the Web of Life and standard systems theory analysis (which covers only the LR quadrant), and beyond a mere embrace of pluralism and diversity (which are confined to the green meme). What is required, they maintain, is an "all-quadrants, all-levels, all-lines" approach. With that, they begin a critique of the past performance of UNICEF and the UN.

> Clearly the process of development must address all four of these quadrants in an integrative fashion if it is to maintain a sustainable direction. But it is equally clear when we look at the evolution of UNICEF's involvement in this process, together with the broader process of human development and how they affect each other, that progress made so far

has largely not produced sustainable change. Attempts to understand the process of change, transformation, or development without an understanding of the nature of the evolution or unfolding of (human) consciousness have little prospect for success.[20]

They then pinpoint a major reason for some of the past failures of UNICEF and the UN. "UNICEF's activities have largely operated in the Upper and Lower Right-Hand quadrants, that is, the quadrants that are objective and exterior (individual and social), and have to a large extent ignored the interior and cultural quadrants." That type of merely Right-Hand approach I have also called "monological" (another word for flatland), and so the analysis proceeds: "Possibly because of an overly monological vision of human development, UNICEF and the UN system have not been successful, or have simply not tried, at any stage, to map the larger picture in which they were involved. This monological vision may well have been necessary in the short term as human consciousness moved through, and is still moving through, the cultural stages of archaic, magic, and mythic, to the rational (and haltingly now to vision-logic or network-logic [i.e., second tier]). But it is now imperative that these organizations adopt a more post or trans-rational approach, one that incorporates positive ideas from the rational level [and, I would add, positive contributions from *all* previous waves], but one that also transcends these to a higher or deeper post-rational level of consciousness, in all of the quadrants."

They then outline the history of UNICEF's various programs, pointing out that, as important as they were, they all focused mostly on Right-Hand initiatives:

- The 1950s was the *Era of Disease Campaigns*: "firmly in the Upper-Right quadrant, that is measurable, observable and objective."
- The 1960s was the *Decade of Development*: "emphasis now on the Lower-Right quadrant, that is, 'functional fit.'"
- The 1970s was the *Era of Alternatives*: "but only alternatives that were mostly Right-Hand quadrants."
- The 1980s was the *Era of Child Survival*: but no mention of interiors or interior development.
- The 1990s was the *Decade of Children's Rights* (all seen in

behavioristic terms), which quickly gave way to the *Era of Donor Fatigue*: "Donors and Governments returned to ['regressed' to] a pre-global state of nationalism stemming from problems at home and a lack of comprehension brought about from the misguided notion of all perspectives being equal [the 'aperspectival madness' of pluralistic relativism]." I have often argued that each holon, in order to survive, needs a balance of justice and rights (agency) with care and responsibilities (communion), and this they echo by saying that the previous efforts of UNICEF and the UN had "no clear juxtaposition of 'rights' (justice) to jurisprudence (care and responsibility) at the global level."

Taking all of these factors into account they conclude that the 2000s are the *Era of the Integral Approach*: "This is where the sustainable process of change is seen from an integrative point of view, which explores more deeply the two Left-Hand quadrants of intention and culture. And of course for UNICEF this will have a major emphasis on children, youths, and women." The problem up to this point is that "all ideas during these five decades were monological to a degree that excluded an understanding of the needs for interior/subjective development in individuals and societies in order to make the process of change and especially transformation sustainable."

They conclude that an "all-quadrants, all-levels, all-lines" approach needs to be taken—carefully and uniquely tailored to each specific situation—in order "to ensure that actions we attempt or programs/ideas/metaphors we propose have any chance of being part of a sustainable, directional, transformative change process."

Let me point out (as do iSchaik Associates) that any such integral approach needs to be implemented with the utmost care, concern, and compassion. None of the levels or lines or quadrants are meant in any sort of rigid, predetermined, judgmental fashion. The point of developmental research is not to pigeonhole people or judge them inferior or superior, but to act as guidelines for *possible potentials that are not being utilized*. The prime directive asks us to honor and appreciate the necessary, vital, and unique contribution provided by each and every wave of consciousness unfolding, and thus act to *protect and promote the health of the entire spiral*, and not any one privileged domain. At the same time, it invites us to offer, as a gentle suggestion, a conception of a more complete spectrum of consciousness, a full spiral of development, so that individuals or cultures (including ours) that are not aware of some of the deeper or higher dimensions of human possibilities may choose to act on those extraordinary resources, which in turn might help to defuse some of the recalcitrant problems that have not yielded to less integral approaches.

THE TERROR OF TOMORROW

One of the greatest problems and constant dangers faced by humanity is simply this: the Right-Hand quadrants are all material, and once a material entity has been produced, it can be used by individuals who are at virtually *any* level of interior development. For example, the atomic bomb is the product of formal-operational thinking (orange), but once it exists, it can be used by individuals at lower levels of development, even though those levels could not themselves produce the bomb. Nobody at a worldcentric level of moral consciousness would happily unleash the atomic bomb, but somebody at a preconventional, red-meme, egocentric level would quite cheerily bomb the hell of pretty much anybody who got in its way.

Stated in more general terms, one of humanity's constant nightmares has been that technological growth in the Right-Hand quadrants has always run ahead of the Left-Hand growth in wisdom, care, and compassionate use of that technology. In other words, exterior development has run ahead of interior development (only because, again, once a material artifact has been produced, it can be used by any interior level; and thus one genius operating at a high cognitive level—James Watt, for example—can conceive and produce a technology—in this case, the steam engine—that can then be used by individuals at any level of development, the vast majority of which could never themselves invent such technology).

Until the modern era, this problem was limited in its means because the technologies themselves were quite limited. You can only inflict so much damage on the biosphere, and on other human beings, with a bow and arrow. But with the emergence of modernity and the orange meme and its sweeping scientific capacities, humanity began producing orange-level technology when most of humanity was still at red or blue levels of moral consciousness. Exterior development, now incredibly powerful, was *not* met with an equal amount of interior development, and as Right-Hand technology ran ahead of Left-Hand wisdom, global catastrophes, for the first time in history, became possible and even likely. From atomic holocaust to ecological suicide, humanity began facing on a massive scale its single most fundamental problem: lack of integral development.

Today, with the rise of powerful second-tier technologies—from quantum-level energy production to artificial intelligence (robotics) to systematic genetic engineering to nanotechnology unleashed on a global scale!—humanity is once again faced with its most primordial nightmare: an explosive growth in Right-Hand technologies has not been met with an equivalent growth in interior consciousness and wisdom. But this time, the lack of integral growth might signal the end of humanity itself.

Bill Joy, cofounder of Sun Microsystems, writing in *Wired* magazine ("Why the Future Doesn't Need Us," April 2000), caused a sensation with his estimate that within fifty years, technological advances in genetics, robotics, and nanotechnology might mean the end of the human species: genetics, in that we might intentionally or accidentally create a White Plague; robotics, in that we will be able to download human consciousness into machines, thus ending humanity as we know it [21]; nanotechnology, in that a "gray goo" (a nanomachine equivalent of the White Plague) could turn the biosphere into dust in a matter of days. Scientists he quoted put the odds at 30 to 50 percent that humanity will not survive the century.

This is obviously an enormously complicated topic, but a few things might be said. First, there are basically only two ways to "control" this technology: external legal enforcement (e.g., banning certain types of research), or internal moral constraint (e.g., an interior growth in collective wisdom that seeks and implements wise use of technology). I believe that eventually some degree of both forms will be necessary, but clearly, we cannot even begin to discuss the interior growth of wisdom and consciousness if we continue to ignore the interiors altogether. We will devise *integral* solutions to these global nightmares or we will very likely perish.

Bill Joy recommends a combination of exterior and interior control. He is in favor of attempting to ban or relinquish some types of research; but he also realizes that even if that were fully possible (which is unlikely, given that knowledge slips around boundaries), it would not really address the fundamental problem, which is the need for a growth in collective wisdom. "Where can we look for a new ethical basis to set our course?" he therefore asks. "I have found the ideas in the book *Ethics for the New Millennium*, by the Dalai Lama, to be very helpful. As is perhaps well known but little heeded, the Dalai Lama argues that the most important thing is for us to conduct our lives with love and compassion for others, and that our societies need to develop a stronger notion of universal responsibility and of our interdependency." Any number of other spiritual leaders, from Christianity to Judaism to Hinduism, might echo those worthy sentiments.

But let us immediately note: we cannot simply recommend love and compassion per se, for those unfold from egocentric to ethnocentric to worldcentric, and do we really want an increase in ethnocentric love? Isn't that exactly the cause of much of these problems? The Nazis loved their families, their race, their extended tribe. This is why most religions, centered on the blue meme, have *caused* wars, not prevented them. Not only have religions caused more wars than any other force in history, they did so in the name of an intense love of God and country. Their love was ethnocentric, dispensed freely to true believers and the chosen people, and death to all the others in the name of that love and compassion.

Surely, by "love and compassion," the Dalai Lama and other leaders are actually calling for postconventional, worldcentric, universal love and compassion. But that is a stage of development reached by less than 30 percent of the world's population, whereas virtually 100 percent of the world's population might soon have access to globally destructive technologies. . . .

Clearly, the interior quadrants have some catching up to do. What good is it to continue to focus on the exterior technological wonders before us—from indefinite life extension to computer/mind interlinks to unlimited zero-point energy to worm-hole intergalactic space travel—if all we carry with us is an egocentric or ethnocentric consciousness? Do we really want to colonize space with red-meme Nazis and the KKK? Do we really want Jack the Ripper living 400 years, zipping around the country in his hypercar, unleashing misogynistic nanorobots? Exterior developments are clearly a concern; how much more so are interior developments—or lack there of. . . .

Edwin Firmage, a recognized authority on constitutional and

international law, who has worked for several decades on the control of nuclear weapons, has written that "Law [exterior legal control] can help, but it leaves you hopelessly short of where we must be. Even if by law you could eliminate all nuclear weapons from the earth by fiat, you don't lobotomize a generation of physicists. You could begin the whole process of arms racing again. How do you change the souls of human beings? You have to go where law can't get you. . . ."[22] You have to go, that is, to the interior quadrants and the growth of the soul, the growth of wisdom, the growth of consciousness, an interior growth in the Left-Hand quadrants that will keep pace with the growth in Right-Hand technologies.[23] And it simply does not matter that this is an impossibly difficult task; the alternative is painfully clear.

Whatever the solutions to these problems, the discussion must surely shift to an integral platform, because anything less than that leaves out fundamental dimensions of the crisis, which will then more likely speed out of control on its merry way to a destiny with death.

INTEGRAL INSTITUTE

All of the approaches in this chapter—from the prosaic to the apocalyptic—are just a few of the areas in which a more integral or all-quadrant, all-level approach is having some immediate applications. There are others I have not mentioned: integral feminism, integral law, integral art and literary theory, even integral prison reform. Some of these approaches have been highlighted in a forthcoming book from Shambhala, assembled by a team of editors headed by Jack Crittenden, and tentatively entitled *Kindred Visions—Ken Wilber and Other Leading Integral Thinkers*, with contributions by Alex Grey, Jim Garrison, Joyce Nielsen, Ed Kowalczyk, T George Harris, Marilyn Schlitz, Georg Feuerstein, Larry Dossey, Jenny Wade, Juan Pascual-Leone, Michael Lerner, James Fadiman, Roger Walsh, Leland van den Daele, Francisco Varela, Robert Shear, George Leonard, Michael Zimmerman, Stan Grof, Father Thomas Keating, Ervin Laszlo, Thomas McCarthy for Jürgen Habermas, Eduardo Mendieta for Karl-Otto Apel, Hameed Ali, Robert Frager, Drexel Sprecher, Lawrence Chickering, Gus diZegera, Elizabeth Debold, Lama Surya Das, Rabbi Zalman Schachter-Shalomi, Mitchell Kapor, Don Beck, Frances Vaughan, Robert Forman, Michael Murphy, Max Velmans, Tony Schwartz, David Chalmers, Susanne Cook-Greuter, Howard Gardner, Robert Kegan, John Searle, and Charles Taylor, among many others. All of these men and women have contributed, in their own significant ways, to a more integral and gracious view of the Kosmos.

Many of the theorists contributing to *Kindred Visions* and many of those presented in this book have joined me in starting Integral Institute. As of this moment we have branches of integral medicine, integral psychology, integral spirituality, integral business, integral ecology, integral education, integral art, and integral politics, with more branches in the planning (media, diplomacy, law). Integral Institute hopes to be a major umbrella organization for genuinely integral studies as well as a conduit for funding integral projects. We intend to open an Integral Center as headquarters for the Institute (in New York and/or San Francisco), and we have already started IntegralMedia with Shambhala. If you are interested in joining the Institute or funding it, please stay tuned to the Shambhala.com website for further announcements.

6

Maps of the Kosmos

In all intellectual debates, both sides tend to be correct
in what they affirm, and wrong in what they deny.
— JOHN STUART MILL

A HOLISTIC INDEXING SYSTEM

B ECAUSE THE HOLONIC MODEL originally arose as an attempt
to coherently account for all quadrants, waves, streams, states,
and realms, one of its claims is to be genuinely comprehensive or
holistic—a genuine Theory of Everything. A by-product of this attempted inclusiveness is a system that is very useful in indexing the
various worldviews, philosophies, religions, and sciences that have
been offered over the years. The idea, again, is not that any one of
these various worldviews has the whole picture (including mine), but
that the more of these worldviews can be seamlessly included in a
larger vision, the more accurate the view of the Kosmos that emerges.
This more encompassing view then acts not only as an aid in individual transformation—which we will address in the next chapter—
but as a *holistic indexing system* for the numerous worldviews
themselves, showing their relation to each other and the irreplaceable
importance of each.[1]

In this chapter, we will focus on these various worldviews and suggest how they can, indeed, be brought together into a more integral
vision or T.O.E. We will also take a careful look at the international
political situation and suggest how a holonic indexing system can

shed considerable light on this most difficult of topics, acting both to clarify our political analyses and to suggest practical courses of national and international political action.

All of the theories presented in this chapter are just that: theories, or maps of the world. As such, they are a useful part of helping us attain a more integral view. At the same time, the basic *capacity* for integral, second-tier thinking does not demand that you master all these different maps. You do not have to memorize the various levels, or know all of the civilization blocks we will discuss, or work on making comprehensive maps yourself. However, that second-tier capacity is exercised and encouraged by engaging these integral maps—maps that embrace "all-quadrants, all-levels, all-lines"— because such maps help open our minds, and thus our hearts, to a more inclusive and compassionate embrace of the Kosmos and all of its inhabitants.

So again, although you do not have to learn the following maps, simply engaging them is an exercise in opening mind and heart. In the next chapter we will turn specifically to integral practice itself, which will awaken your own integral capacities in an even more concrete, unmistakable fashion.

WORLDVIEWS

There have been countless attempts, over the years, to categorize the various worldviews that are available to men and women. Plato offered brilliant accounts of the alternative philosophies present in ancient Greece. The Fa-hsiang school categorized the religious systems existing in T'ang China. Saint Thomas Aquinas gave exhaustive representations of the most influential of the existing philosophies— to name just a few.

With the modern era and the understanding of evolution, many theorists began to give classifications of various worldviews in terms of their *development*. One of the first, and still most influential, was that of Auguste Comte, founder of positivism, whose famous "Law of Three" stated that humanity's knowledge quest has gone through three major stages—religion, metaphysics, and science—with each stage being less primitive and more accurate (resulting, by happy chance, in the stage occupied by Comte. The constant downside of developmental theories is that the highest stage is usually, by strange coincidence, evidenced by the proponent of the theory. I hasten to point out that I have never made such a claim myself, though I am often accused of it). By far the most sophisticated of these developmental classifications of knowledge was that of Georg Hegel, whose undeniably brilliant systematic philosophy found room, he believed, for every major worldview in history, Western or Eastern. (Unfortunately, as Bertrand Russell pointed out, all that Hegel actually knew about China, for example, was that it existed. This, and subtler problems with the Hegelian system, brought it tumbling down; but we can nonetheless admire Idealism for the brilliance of what it did manage to accomplish.)[2] Other well-known developmental-historical models (which may involve both growth and decay) include those of Adam Smith, Karl Marx, Herbert Spencer, Oswald Spengler, Arnold Toynbee, Pitirim Sorokin, Antonio Gramsci, Teilhard de Chardin, Carroll Quigley, Jürgen Habermas, Gerhard Lenski, Jean Gebser, and Sri Aurobindo.

More recently, certain philosophers have attempted "overview" models that suggest the *types* of worldviews that people *can* form. One of the first was Stephen C. Pepper's *World Hypotheses* (1942), which claimed there are four of them: formistic (the world exists as categories), mechanistic (the world is cause–effect), contextual (the world is relational), and organismic (the world is interactive and relational). Schwartz and Russek (see the section "Integral Medicine" in chap. 5), building on Pepper, added four more: implicit process (the world has subtler energies and consciousness), circular causality (cybernetic), creative unfolding (emergent adaptation), and integrative diversity (which attempts to integrate them all).[3]

Another influential classification of worldviews according to available types was that of social systems theorist Talcott Parsons, who laid out worldviews along a (political) continuum of five major positions: Right Systemist, Right Marginalist, Middle Marginalist, Left Marginalist, Left Systemist. Although this has some utility, it actually covers a very narrow, middle-level range of possible worldviews, as we will see. Robert Bellah has cut his analysis at another angle, finding four major worldviews in America: republican, biblical, utilitarian, and romantic. Mark Gerzon finds six: religious, capitalist, disaffected, media, new age, and political. Samuel P. Huntington sees the world dominated by a clash of nine major cultural worldviews (or civilizations): Western, Latin American,

African, Islamic, Sinic, Hindu, Orthodox, Buddhist, and Japanese. But those are all good examples of the "meta-analysis" of types of worldviews that many modern scholars have found useful—and they *are* useful, provided we can find a more encompassing context from which all can be accorded some sort of respect. (Ah, and there's the rub.)

The notion of *levels* of reality (or waves of existence) brings yet another kind of indexing system. Whether we use Spiral Dynamics, or the Great Chain of Being, or Jane Loevinger's levels of self, the point is that we can rather easily classify types of worldviews according *to the level of the worldview itself*, and numerous theorists have done exactly that. To give a few quick examples: sexual and vital worldviews, such as Freud and Bergson, are said to stem predominantly from the level of biological life, or the beige meme; power worldviews, such as Nietzsche, from the red meme; rational worldviews, such as Descartes, from orange; postmodernism, such as Derrida and Lyotard, green; nature mysticism, such as Thoreau, coral/psychic; deity mysticism, such as Saint Teresa of Avila, subtle; and formless mysticism, such as Meister Eckhart, causal.[4]

It seems quite reasonable that levels of being and knowing indeed contribute to the existence of various worldviews; hence it might be wise to include this fact in any genuine T.O.E.

There is one final requirement. An integral synthesis, to be truly integral, must find a way that all of the major worldviews are basically *true* (even though partial). It is not that the higher levels are giving more accurate views, and the lower levels are giving falsity, superstition, or primitive nonsense. There must be a sense in which even "childish" magic and Santa Claus myths are true. For those worldviews are simply the way *the world looks at that level*, or from that wave, and *all* of the waves are crucial ingredients of the Kosmos. At the mythic level, Santa Claus (or Zeus or Apollo or astrology) is a phenomenological reality. It will do no good to say, "Well, we have evolved beyond that stage, and so now we know that Santa Claus is not real," because if that is true—and all stages are shown to be primitive and false in light of further evolution—then we will have to admit that our own views, *right now*, are also false (because future evolution will move beyond them). But it is not that there is *one* level of reality, and those other views are all primitive and *incorrect* versions of that one level. Each of those views is a *correct* view of a lower yet fundamentally important level of reality, not an incorrect view of the one real level. The notion of *development* allows us to recognize nested truths, not primitive superstitions.[5]

I am often asked, why even attempt an integration of the various worldviews? Isn't it enough to simply celebrate the rich diversity of various views and not try to integrate them? Well, recognizing diversity is certainly a noble endeavor, and I heartily support that pluralism. But if we remain merely at the stage of celebrating diversity, we ultimately are promoting fragmentation, alienation, separation and despair. You go your way, I go my way, we both fly apart—which is often what has happened under the reign of the pluralistic relativists, who have left us a postmodern Tower of Babel on too many fronts. It is not enough to recognize the many ways in which we are all different; we need to go further and start recognizing the many ways that we are also similar. Otherwise we simply contribute to heapism, not wholism. Building on the rich diversity offered by pluralistic relativism, we need to take the next step and weave those many strands into a holonic spiral of unifying connections, an interwoven Kosmos of mutual intermeshing. We need, in short, to move from pluralistic relativism to universal integralism—we need to keep trying to find the One-in-the-Many that is the form of the Kosmos itself.

That, I believe, is why we should attempt these types of integrative visions. Will we ever completely succeed? Never. Should we keep trying? Always. Why? Because an intention to find the One-in-the-Many aligns our hearts and heads with the One-in-the-Many that is Spirit itself as its shines in the world, radiantly.

I believe that such an integral approach is the most viable attempt to represent the One-in-the-Many, because it explicitly embraces and honors all of the worldview conceptions mentioned in this chapter (as we will see). This integral overview or Theory of Everything further acts, as I suggested, as an indexing system for all these worldviews, thus allowing us to appreciate the special and profound contribution that each makes. And, it goes without saying, my own version of this T.O.E., even if it were completely true, is destined only to pass into yet further, better visions.

This integral indexing system is already being used in several applications, from "transformational websites" to "world libraries." The World Economic Forum in Davos, Switzerland, recently invited several panels on an "all-quadrant, all-level" approach, which is perhaps an indication of its pragmatic usefulness.

ROBERT BELLAH, MARK GERZON

If we use *quadrants, levels, lines, types,* and *states,* there is ample room for all of the worldviews mentioned in this chapter. This is actually much simpler than it sounds. Let's look at some concrete examples.

Many of the various worldview theorists focus on one quadrant and outline its major stages and/or types (fig. 3-6, page 51, gave several examples of this common "one-quadrant" phenomenon). Robert Bellah, for example, focuses on the Lower-Left quadrant and two of its major levels: the mythic-membership (blue), with two of its principal types (republican and biblical), and the egoic-rational (orange), with two of its principal types (utilitarian and therapeutic; a subset of therapeutic is green). His analysis, I believe, is a fine sociological description of these four level-types in the Lower-Left quadrant, although his prescriptions are perhaps too heavily weighted toward blue.[6]

Gerzon's analysis finds six major "nations" or "belief systems" existing in America today: religious, capitalist, disaffected, media, new age, and political—which mean pretty much just what the names suggest. His analysis, conducted largely through the green meme (a wonderful pluralistic sensitivity), is another useful descriptive phenomenology of some of the major worldviews present in America (whose correlations I will outline in an endnote).[7] Notice that all of those "nations" are first tier; there are no second-tier nations or major centers of population around which second-tier organizations might fruitfully emerge (the Gaia or "transformation" nation is heavily green/purple/red, with an extremely small minority—less than 2 percent—actively engaged in second-tier and higher concerns). Yet without a second-tier operating base, the "new patriotism" that Gerzon wisely recommends will probably remain sporadic at best.

VERTICAL DEPTH

The classification scheme of Talcott Parsons, useful as it is, is an example of the limitations that result when multi-level phenomena are not taken into account. Parsons's continuum (Right Systemist, Right Marginalist, Middle Marginalist, Left Marginalist, Left Systemist) is an example of a few of the types of worldviews that can be seen *from* the rational levels—they are all rational worldviews. That spectrum of views is not a *vertical* scale reaching above or below the rational levels but a *horizontal* scale within them, stretching from systemic belief in interior causation (Right Systemist) to systemic belief in exterior causation (Left Systemist). As we saw in chapter 3, each level of consciousness has various horizontal types available to it. *Political orientation* is a *type* that is available at several *levels* (you can be Left or Right red, Left or Right blue, Left or Right orange, etc.).[8] The point is that these are independent scales: horizontal levels versus the various typologies available within various levels.

Parsons's scheme is predominantly a horizontal typology from within the egoic-rational waves. This is why his scheme does not cover (or even recognize) the extremely important worldviews that are seen *from* the archaic wave (beige), the magical wave (purple), and the mythic wave (red/blue)—waves that contain up to 70 percent of the world's population, all missed by Parsons! (Not to mention the higher, transmental, transpersonal waves of psychic, subtle, and causal, to which we will return in a moment.)

What is lacking in Parsons's scheme is, of course, *the vertical dimension of depth* that we will see is generally missing in all of the conventional theorists discussed in this chapter.[9] In fact, all of the theorists in this chapter (except Evelyn Underhill) are coming mostly *from* the rational level(s), and they give us a series of extremely useful worldviews from that perspective. But, as we will continue to see, we need to supplement their important but limited perspectives with a more all-quadrant, all-level view, especially when it comes to the higher stages themselves, and more importantly, to the *early stages* of development (purple, red, and blue) that so dominate the world's population.

FRANCIS FUKUYAMA:
The End of History and the Last Man

Three of the most influential analysts of world affairs today are Francis Fukuyama, Samuel Huntington, and, on a popular level, Thomas Friedman. The differences between them are illustrative of the different emphases they give to the various quadrants, levels, and lines. Fukuyama (*The End of History and the Last Man*) stresses the egoic-rational level (orange) and its *need for self-recognition* (in Maslow's needs hierarchy, the self-esteem needs). He notes that the liberal-economic state has managed to deliver this mutual recognition more effectively than any other system in history. He thus believes that no further major historical changes can or will occur in that regard, so that the liberal West, in that sense, has won history, thus "ending" it.

There are many important truths in what Fukuyama says. The problem is that his analysis holds only for the egoic-rational, post-conventional, worldcentric levels (orange and green), which, as we have seen, constitute around 30 percent of the world's population. Moreover, every person around the world—even those born in an egoic-rational, liberal, postconventional nation—starts existence at stage 1 (archaic, beige), and must migrate through the spiral of development, a development that, five or six major stages later, will eventuate in a postconventional (orange) consciousness. *But less than a third of the world's population does so*—due to factors in all four quadrants—and thus the rest of the world (or some 70 percent of its population) does not share Mr. Fukuyama's love of, or even recognition of, the egoic-rational wave (orange), but prefers variations on archaic, magic, and mythic (purple, red, and blue). Thus, Fukuyama anchors his analysis in the orange meme of the Left-Hand quadrant and in liberal-capitalistic economic factors in the Lower-Right quadrant, but that leaves out the pre-orange stages of development that hold the majority of the world's population.

SAMUEL P. HUNTINGTON: *The Clash of Civilizations*

This is where Samuel Huntington's analysis is extremely useful. For "underneath" the worldcentric, postconventional, orange and green memes, there lie the roots and foundations of the various ethnocentric civilizations (including our own). Although many of these ethnocentric civilizations contain worldcentric ideals, nonetheless the masses of people in each civilization remain heavily in the purple, red, blue (and more rarely, orange) waves of consciousness unfolding. Huntington's analysis gives nine of these huge *civilization blocks:* Western, Latin American, African, Islamic, Sinic, Hindu, Orthodox, Buddhist, and Japanese (see fig. 6-1). These are the hori-

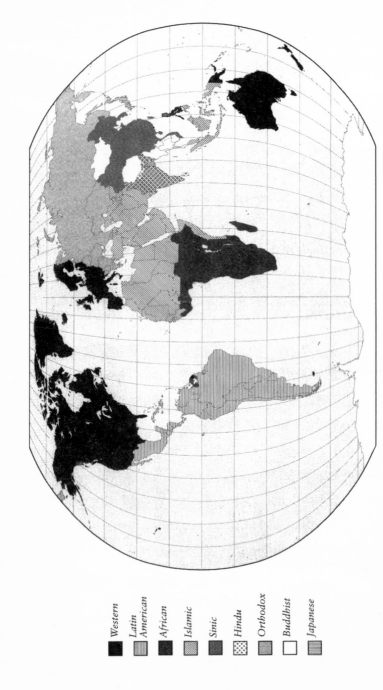

Western

Latin
American

African

Islamic

Sinic

Hindu

Orthodox

Buddhist

Japanese

Figure 6-1. Civilization Blocks. Adapted, by permission, from Samuel P. Huntington, The Clash of Civilizations and the Remaking of World Order (New York: Simon & Schuster, 1996, pp. 26–27).

zontal tectonic plates, as it were, of human culture, and taking them into account is absolutely crucial. These plates, Huntington persuasively argues, are some of the primary motivators in international politics, commerce, war, and diplomacy.[10]

As we will see, although Huntington gives a fairly broad definition of civilizations, he is especially focusing on the Lower-Left quadrant, or *culture* in the specific sense.[11] And his recommendations are heavily weighted to the blue meme, or a conservative-republican stance (which is not necessarily as bad as many liberals would have us believe: remember, 70 percent of the world's population is blue or lower, and thus, when in Rome. . . . Moreover, as we saw, conservatives—precisely because they recognize interior causation and stages of the interior up to blue—are often much more reliable and realistic judges of those interior domains than are liberals, who usually don't acknowledge them at all and thus are literally flying blind through the interior territories while demanding exterior changes.)

For most of humanity's history, the Left- and Right-Hand quadrants developed lockstep with each other. In the Lower Left, the evolution from archaic (beige) to magic (purple) to mythic (red/blue) to rational (orange) was accompanied in the Lower Right by technological development that moved, respectively, from foraging to horticultural to agrarian to industrial (see fig. 4-4). Magical worldviews went with a foraging base, mythic worldviews went with an agrarian base, rational worldviews went with an industrial base, and so on.

But with the rise of modernity (rational-industrial), the increasing globalization of economic exchange made a very intense type of *cross-level* phenomenon possible: for example, tribal cultures could gain access to rational-industrial technology, often with horrifying results. Moreover, the same sort of cross-level access could occur *within* a given culture: Auschwitz was the product of rational-technological capacity (orange) pressed into the hands of intensely prerational (red/blue) ethnocentric aggression. Today, almost any ethnic tribe or feudal order can gain access to nuclear, biological, and chemical weapons that historically they would never have been able to produce themselves, and the results are literally explosive. As we began to note in the previous chapter, precisely because the Right-Hand quadrants are all *material*, these material artifacts (modes of technology to nuclear weapons) can be obtained by individuals at almost *any* level of interior, Left-Hand development, even if they themselves could never produce them. These types of phenomena make cross-level analysis of quadrants, levels, and lines absolutely mandatory in today's world politics, and it dooms analyses that do less than that. (We will return to this important topic later in the discussion.)

The essential point is simply that civilizations evidence, in part, the pyramid of development, where the higher the level of development, the fewer individuals at it. This means that the bulk of the world's population, as we were saying, is at the early or foundational waves—primarily purple, red, and blue (and more rarely, orange). That is not a moral judgment; not only do all of those stages perform crucial functions in every culture, they are the necessary foundation stones for further development. As we said, every person, in every culture, no matter how "high" or "advanced," is born at square 1 and begins the great unfolding from there. The prime directive is thus to act in ways that, to the best of our judgment, will protect and promote the health of the entire spiral of development, and not to unduly privilege a favorite wave.

But this does mean that a new "realpolitik" will take into account the entire Spiral, while realizing that the bulk of the population will remain at purple/red (preconventional) and blue (conventional). Thus the bulk of the world's population is egocentric-to-ethnocentric, and these ethnocentric blocks will have an enormous hand in shaping world currents (just as Huntington says). Not the only hand, as we will see, but a very important one. As we saw in chapter 1, Beck and Cowan estimate that 10 percent of the world's population is purple, 20 percent red, and 40 percent blue—thus around 70 percent of the world's population has a center of gravity at ethnocentric or lower: an extraordinary mass of humanity.

That also means that around 70 percent of the world's population falls short of the level at which Fukuyama's analysis would kick in. (When close to 100 percent of the world's population can be expected to reach orange in their lifetimes, that might be a type of "end of history" according to Fukuyama's criteria—but that is a century or two away, if then. Besides, there is then green, then yellow, then turquoise, then coral/psychic. . . . It appears, alas, that history might never end. . . .)

VERTICAL AND HORIZONTAL

Unfortunately Huntington's analysis, brilliant and useful up to a point, is largely conducted on a horizontal playing field. He recognizes the existence and profound importance of these large civilization blocks, but he does not acknowledge the vertical levels of development (e.g., purple, red, blue, orange, green, yellow) that are some of the crucial *archeological strata* of these blocks. He is giving us a surface reading of the very real territories that are today present, but he is not giving us the deep developmental analysis of the infrastructures of those blocks. Adding this vertical dimension to his horizontal analysis—recognizing not only the tectonic plates but the archeological levels in those plates—will give us a much more integral perspective from which to make sounder political judgments.

Let me give a few examples of what this all-quadrant, all-level approach might involve. Figure 6-2 is a diagram from Don Beck and Graham Linscott's *The Crucible: Forging South Africa's Future.* It shows the average memetic mix in the adult population of the United States, Europe, Sub-Saharan Africa, and South Africa. Adding this kind of vertical analysis to Huntington's horizontal analysis would give us a more three-dimensional, integral index of what is actually

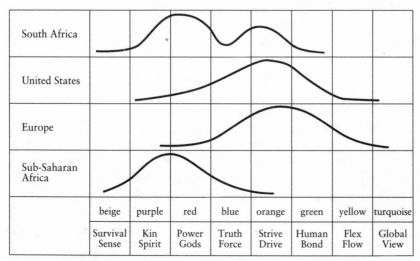

	beige	purple	red	blue	orange	green	yellow	turquoise
	Survival Sense	Kin Spirit	Power Gods	Truth Force	Strive Drive	Human Bond	Flex Flow	Global View

Figure 6-2. Value Systems Mosaics. Adapted, by permission, from Don Beck and Graham Linscott, The Crucible: Forging South Africa's Future *(Johannesburg, South Africa: The New Paradigm Press, 1991, pp. 80–81).*

going on in various populations—politically, militarily, culturally, and so on.

(Beck made over sixty trips to South Africa, working with those who were dismantling apartheid. Liberals, of course, usually maintain that "stages" or "levels" are marginalizing and oppressive, but in fact that is only true of the misuse of stage conceptions, and then only by people who would try to oppress others anyway, whether using hierarchical stages or antihierarchical political correctness. Beck has been tireless in pointing out that stage conceptions correctly used actually help to free people from racial stereotypes: "There are not black and white people; there are purple people, blue people, orange people, green people. . . ." Small wonder that he was commended by both Nelson Mandela and Zulu leader Mongosuthu Buthelezi for his innovative work in this area.)

Several items stand out immediately in this diagram. Europe and America have a center of gravity at orange, with strong pockets of blue and green (most of the "culture wars," in fact, are blue conservatives fighting with green liberals, as I try to point out in *Boomeritis*). Sub-Saharan Africa is still centered in purple-to-red tribal consciousness. Northern Africa and much of the Mid-East is dominated by strong blue patriarchies and feudal orders (based largely on the narrow-religion aspects of the Koran). Huntington's horizontal civilization blocks thus actually contain vertical memetic structures as well, and taking both of these dimensions into account seems essential.

South Africa was a particularly difficult situation precisely because it was a clash of both different *horizontal* civilizations (European and Sub-Saharan African) and different *vertical* meme structures (purple/red vs. blue/orange). Apartheid itself was a typically blue-structure arrangement. (Dominator social hierarchies in both the West and the East—from apartheid to the caste system—are found almost exclusively in blue, mythic-membership structures.) On this blue foundation, the whites in South Africa had built a strong, orange, capitalistic state. When apartheid was taken down—very abruptly, and with perhaps little thought as to what would replace it—South Africa was thrown into turmoil. Of course apartheid needed to be dismantled, but South Africans needed a little more time to grow a blue structure *of their own* that could replace the European version. Beck, who has remained close to South African leaders, says that this is proceeding haltingly, in difficult fits and starts. (It has not been helped by green liberals who, with the standard lack of belief in interior stages, have simply insisted that all blue structures be dismantled, which has crippled the overall spiral.)

As with South Africa, many of the truly difficult international situations are the result of both clashing civilization blocks (on the horizontal scale) and warring memes (on the vertical). Vietnam was an endless quagmire of two clashing civilizations (Sinic and Western) at different developmental levels (red/blue and orange/green), with the result that the corporate state of America was mired in the mud of ancient nations and feudal empires.

The Serbian conflict has been an absolute nightmare because there is a violent clash of at least three civilization blocks (Orthodox, Islamic, Western) spanning at least four developmental levels (purple ethnic tribes, red feudal empires, blue ancient nations, and orange/green states). Slobodan Milosevic has taken the blue ancient nation of Serbia and unleashed red-tribal ethnic cleansing, rape, and torture. Sensitive-green liberals Bill Clinton and Tony Blair have intervened in an attempt to protect green human rights, an attempt that has fallen on deaf ears in the blue ancient nations of Russia, China, and Iran, who consider both Clinton and Blair to be the real war criminals (and from their meme structure, that is perfectly understandable). Nothing substantial has changed in the area; the tectonic plates and memes are still juxtaposed in extremely unstable fashion, ready for the next earthquake.

The important role of vertical waves or memes can be further seen in the reunification of Germany. The German peoples share the same civilization block, the same genetic pool, and much of the same history. Yet, due to the events during the Cold War, East Germany fell under the dominance of a Marxist fundamentalist state power—in essence, a blue ancient nation, with one-party rule and obedience to the state; while West Germany continued its development into an orange corporate state with strong green elements. Reunification has thus been predominantly a problem of meshing these two quite different cultural-developmental waves (blue vs. orange/green). Of course, lurking in the background of both Germanys is the temporary insanity of the World-War-II regression to purple/red ethnic cleansing and the Holocaust, waged with extremely powerful orange technology: the peculiar cross-level nightmare made possible by modernity. The difficulties faced in the reunification of Germany are not due to a horizontal clash of civilizations but to a vertical clash of memes.

Likewise with the Soviet Union. Although ostensibly a modern state, its infrastructure was more substantially that of a blue ancient nation, with totalitarian rule, one-party dominance, command economies, and collectivistic ideals. Because an orange-meme, individual-initiative-driven, capitalistic market cannot develop under those circumstances, when something resembling a market economy was rather abruptly introduced, the ancient nation did not evolve forward into an orange modern state but in many ways regressed back to a red feudal empire, rife with warring gangs, criminal warloads, and a Russian mafia that controls much of the market. This has been accompanied by correlative Lower-Right-quadrant structural deficits, as an ancient nation continues its difficult development into a modern state. Needless to say, at this moment green human rights are the last of its worries or interests.

A similar cultural-developmental struggle is occurring in mainland China, where a blue ancient nation is ratcheting in fits and starts toward an orange modern state. Generally speaking, this development is not helped by making green human rights the main issue. Blue nations intuitively (and correctly) understand that green human rights will corrosively dissolve blue structure, and that spells disaster for China. Only as an orange infrastructure—with its growing middle class, its technology, its respect for objective human rights, and its freeing of individual initiative—begins to take root, do green human rights have any meaning at all, let alone appeal. Even if a blue nation wanted to move to green pluralism, it structurally could not do so, and thus pressing the issue simply tends to increase reactionary and paranoid responses.

All of this goes to point up a central fact of civilizations and their discontents: only with correlative interior developments can exterior developments be implemented and sustained. It is not that one is more important than the other, but that they rise and fall together. An all-quadrant, all-level analysis gives us purchase on this primordial issue.

THE MEAN GREEN MEME

Although Huntington's analysis is bereft of vertical depth, he gives a fine analysis of how the horizontal civilization blocks are some of the prime factors in international politics, commerce, cultural intercourse, and war. The entire analysis—highly recommended—is testament to the fact that, in the great spiral of development from egocentric to ethnocentric to worldcentric, the bulk of the world's population is ethnocentric, and will likely so remain for the indefinite future (as it has been for millennia). This is not to say that worldcentric cultures cannot or will not emerge—in fact, Huntington sees some evidence of this happening now (as we will see)—only that the center of gravity in the various civilization blocks is heavily ethnocentric, and, due to the pyramid of development, these ethnocentric clusters will always be powerful (and often dominant) factors in individual and cultural consciousness.

Huntington then moves to his policy recommendations, and there is no question about it: they are heavily blue meme (a general republican-conservative view of the world). This has often infuriated liberals (and the green meme), because it violates their stated aims of diversity, multiculturalism, and sensitivity. But once again, as with Fukuyama's analysis, the liberal-green analysis only applies to a very small percentage of the world's population. In fact, Beck and Cowan have found that less than 10 percent of the world's population is at green (and almost all of that is in the Western civilization block, which is a massive embarrassment for the green multiculturalists, who champion everything *except* Western civilization).

Moreover, in order for the rest of the world to get to green, individuals have to develop from purple to red to blue to orange to green. As Beck and Cowan (and virtually all developmental researchers) constantly stress, the blue meme (by whatever name) is an absolutely crucial, unavoidable, necessary building block of the higher stages (including green), and yet green does virtually everything in its power to destroy blue wherever it finds it. As Spiral Dynamics puts it, "Green dissolves blue"—and in so doing, as Beck himself says, "Green has introduced more harm in the last thirty years than any other meme."

It is not that what green is saying is wrong; it is simply a case of very bad timing. The world at large—and much of America—is simply not ready for green pluralism. More than that, as Huntington quite correctly points out, no civilization in history has survived with a pluralistic agenda—but not because, as Huntington believes, no civilization can so survive, but simply that, until more than 10 percent of the population is actually at the green wave, then the cultural center of gravity will be heavily pre-green, and thus a culture that tries to ram pluralism and multiculturalism down everybody's throat is going to come apart at the seams faster than you can say "deconstruction." That is what Beck means by saying that the harm green has done has often outweighed the good—and that is what Huntington is also sharply criticizing.

The difference, however—and this is a big however—is that Beck is giving a post-green analysis, based on the prime directive: namely, when green dissolves blue, it cripples the spiral of development. It makes it absolutely impossible for purple and red to develop further, because there is no blue base to accept the development. Green is thus horribly damaging the overall spiral of human unfolding, here and abroad, and thus erasing much of the undeniable good that green can, and has, done on its own. The prime directive is for all of the memes, including blue and green, to be seen as necessary parts of the overall spiral, and thus each be allowed to make its own crucial contribution to the comprehensive health of the spiral.

Huntington, on the other hand, is giving something of a pre-green attack on green. He is championing blue because he does not like green. (He is not attacking the notion of what might be called "international pluralism," which recognizes the importance and legitimacy of the major civilization blocks—in fact, Huntington is a strong advocate of international pluralism. He is attacking multiculturalism in America, which he feels is dissolving certain necessary foundations.) This has made many liberals completely ignore the important points of Huntington's argument. Nonetheless, even if Huntington's recommendations are heavily blue, that is often where we need to *begin* in many instances. Green has, inadvertently or not, damaged blue infrastructures both here and abroad, and a structural refurbishing is wisely in order (reversing what George W. Bush has called "the soft bigotry of lowered expectations").

On a sturdy blue and then orange foundation, green ideals can be built. No blue and orange, no green. Thus green's attack on blue and orange is profoundly suicidal. Not only that, but when the highly developed, postformal green wave champions any and every "multicultural" movement, it acts to *encourage* other memes *not* to grow into green. The more green succeeds, the more it destroys itself. Thus, it is to green's great advantage to adopt the prime directive and work for ways to facilitate the entire spiral of development, and not adopt order-Left imperatives commanding everybody to be sensitive.

The green meme—which constitutes approximately 20 percent of adult American population and is the core of Paul Ray's misnamed "integral culture"—now has a chance to move into second-tier and genuinely integral constructions. The green meme has been in charge of academia, the cultural elite, and much of liberal politics for the past three decades, but it is now being challenged on all sides (its internal self-contradictions, its failed political agenda, the harsh intolerance of the politically correct thought police, its claim to be superior in a world where nothing is supposed to be superior, the nihilism and narcissism of extreme postmodernism, an aggressive marginalization of holarchies and thus its lack of an integral vision). As happens when any meme begins to lose its hegemony, its Inquisitors begin an often belligerent and reactionary defense—what might be called in this case "the mean green meme" (which is especially the home of boomeritis). And it is boomeritis and the MGM that are now some of the primary roadblocks to a truly integral, more inclusive approach. Whether the hegemony of the MGM crumbles within the next decade or two—leaving behind the many positive, important, necessary functions of the healthy green meme—or whether it holds on bitterly until the death of its adherents (the expected course if history is any judge) remains to be seen.

Nonetheless, the more people at the green wave, the more people are ready to make the leap into the hyperspace of second-tier consciousness, where truly integral approaches to the world's problems can be conceived and implemented.

WORLD CIVILIZATION

Huntington ends his blue discussion with the recognition of the emergence of a postconventional, worldcentric, World Civilization (Huntington uses a capital "C" in this case), which is just now slowly beginning, and which not only partakes of orange/green, but begins to intuit the integral, second-tier waves—a type of integral, global, World Civilization. Huntington's recommendations do not stem from that level, but he does recognize it, and he recognizes that the world is slowly moving in that integral direction.

Huntington notes that what is often called "universalism" is really just imperialism; that is, one civilization (such as Western) tries to impose its values on all the others. That is a universalism that

Huntington and I both categorically reject. But Huntington moves toward a universalism of "commonalities," which means that, in addition to recognizing and honoring the many important differences between cultures, we also attempt to cherish those things that we have in common as human beings living on a very small planet, a healthy universalism I strongly share (what I also call unity-in-diversity, universal pluralism, unitas multiplex, universal integralism, etc.). "In a multicivilizational world," says Huntington, "the constructive course is to renounce universalism [imperialism], accept diversity [international pluralism], and seek commonalities [healthy universalism]." I quite agree, as far as that goes.

As for a healthy universalism and World Civilization—an integral Civilization—Huntington concludes, correctly I believe, that "if human beings are ever to *develop a universal civilization*, it will emerge gradually through the exploration and expansion of these commonalities. Thus . . . , peoples in all civilizations should search for and attempt to expand the values, institutions, and practices they have in common with peoples of other civilizations."

He then moves toward the heart of the matter, the transformation from ethnocentric (blue) to worldcentric (and integral): "This effort would contribute not only to limiting the clash of civilizations but also to strengthening Civilization in the singular [not imperialism but healthy universalism]. The singular Civilization presumably refers to a complex mix of *higher levels* of morality, religion, learning, art, philosophy, technology, material well-being, and probably other things" (italics added). In other words, as I would put it, the various developmental lines or streams (morality, religion, learning, art, etc.) move through the developmental levels or waves (purple, red, blue, orange, green, etc.—or, in short, egocentric to ethnocentric to worldcentric), and the higher the level of development in the various lines, the greater the chance for the emergence of a World Civilization— precisely because the tectonic plates do in fact move from egocentric to ethnocentric to worldcentric. Huntington's analysis reminds us that the vast bulk of the world's population is still ethnocentric, and a realpolitik had better take that into account if it wants to actually reach a worldcentric anything.

At the same time, a worldcentric Civilization is not a uniform, imperialistic, homogenized mush, but a rich tapestry of unity-in-diversity, with as much emphasis on the diversity as on the unity. What it does not do is champion *only* ethnocentric diversity, which leads to all the horrors—fragmentation, alienation, and war—that Huntington so devastatingly chronicles.

Huntington then raises the crucial question to which his entire book has pointed: "How can one chart the ups and downs of humanity's development of Civilization?" He asks the question, and then the book ends.

My own suggestion, of course, is that an "all-quadrant, all-level, all-lines" approach is one of the best methods available for charting that extraordinary unfolding from egocentric to ethnocentric to worldcentric, in all its perilous ups and downs, thus making more friendly the waters leading to the promised land of worldcentric Civilization and unitas multiplex. And that is not a final end point, but simply a new beginning.

Thomas L. Friedman:
The Lexus and the Olive Tree

Thomas L. Friedman, though considered by some to be a mere popularizer, manages to put his finger on several items that the other analysts either miss or fail to emphasize. Unfortunately, his overview is also a strictly surface or horizontal affair, consisting of six major domains or streams, but bereft of any levels or waves. (This flatland approach, which ignores the crucially important waves of development, is not peculiar to Friedman but, as we have seen throughout this chapter, is the standard approach in most of today's political and sociocultural analyses, including those of Huntington, Zbigniew Brzezinski, Paul Kennedy, Robert Kaplan, etc., much as their work is otherwise truly admirable, and much as their partial truths need to be fully included in any integral analysis).

Friedman's six domains or streams are: politics, culture, national security, finance, technology, and environment; and he maintains that in order to understand one of them, you have to try to understand all of them. He then congratulates Paul Kennedy and John Lewis Gaddis for also attempting to be more "integral" and "global," and as much as I half-applaud that move, the "global" they recommend is global flatland, the flatland Web of Life, which is interconnected on one level, but completely lacks vertical depth. "In an essay they jointly authored," says Friedman, "Gaddis and Kennedy bemoaned the fact that particularists are too often, in too many countries, the ones still making and analyzing foreign policy. 'These people,' the two Yale historians wrote, 'are perfectly competent at taking in parts of the picture, but they have difficulty seeing the entire thing. They pigeonhole priorities, pursuing them separately and simultaneously, with little thought to how each might undercut the other. They proceed confidently enough from tree to tree, but seem astonished to find themselves lost in the forest. The great strategists of the past kept forests as well as the trees in view. They were generalists, and they operated from an ecological perspective. They understood that the world is a web, in which adjustments made here are bound to have effects over there—that everything is interconnected. Where, though, might one find generalists today? . . . The dominant trend within universities and the think tanks is toward ever-narrower specialization: a higher premium is placed on functioning deeply within a single field than broadly across several. And yet without some awareness of the whole . . . , there can be no strategy. And without strategy, there is only drift.'"

And without depth, there is even more drift. All of those theorists—including Kennedy, Gaddis, and Friedman—focus almost entirely on the Lower-Right quadrant (including systems theory, chaos and complexity theories, web of life, flatland holism, techno-economic globalization, etc.). They either ignore the Left-Hand quadrants or, if they acknowledge them in passing, fail to recognize the vertical levels of developmental depth in those crucial quadrants. They thus commit subtle reductionism—reducing all Left-Hand events to Right-Hand functional fit—and present a flatland holism (Right-Hand only) and not an integral holism (both Left- and Right-Hand realities).[12]

What needs to be added to flatland holism and the ecological Web of Life is the vertical depth dimension and the pyramid of life: *both* dimensions are profoundly important. An analysis that is bereft of the vertical dimension of the waves of consciousness unfolding is playing flatland chess, not three-dimensional chess (which happens to be the game the real world is playing), and thus the crucial height and depth dimensions slip through the analysis, so that the analysis, by default, *proceeds from the level of the subjective development of the analyst*. This usually means that the blue, orange, or green meme tries to understand the entire spiral of development through the lens of its own level, with less than satisfactory results.

So although I applaud the "Web of Life" interconnections (two quadrants, no levels) that these analysts are bringing to the picture, I suggest that a more adequate conception (all quadrants, all levels) would serve strategy with even less drift.[13]

To return to Friedman. The title of his recent book, *The Lexus and the Olive Tree*, is meant to indicate what he sees as one of the fundamental conflicts in today's world: the tension between specific cultures (similar to Huntington's "civilizations"), which are local, and increasing globalization, which is not. Techno-economic globalization (represented by the Lexus) tends to disrupt, even destroy, local traditions and cultures (represented by the olive tree), and that clash is a central factor in today's world. Friedman gives an overview of the six domains and how they play out in this central conflict, but the star of his narrative, and what he believes is a major driving force, is that of global technology, from the Lexus to cyberspace, for it is proceeding with what appears to be its own relentless logic: homogenize the world. But, like it or not, globalization is here to stay: "I believe that if you want to understand the post-Cold War world you have to start by understanding that a new international system has succeeded it—globalization. That is 'The One Big Thing' people should focus on. Globalization is not the only thing influencing events in the world today, but to the extent that there is North Star and a worldwide shaping force, it is this system. What is new is the system; what is old is power politics, chaos, clashing civilizations, and liberalism. And what is the drama of the post-Cold War world is the interaction between this new system and these old passions."

Friedman's analysis of globalization, while recognizing many streams, concentrates almost entirely on those in the Lower-Right quadrant: the social system of techno-economic globalization that is pulling the rest of the train. As far as his Lower-Right quadrant analysis goes, I believe he is generally correct (but, as we will see, the lack of recognition of vertical depth in the interior quadrants hobbles the analysis). His conclusions (at least in the LR) are also in line with the analysis, controversial at the time but now more accepted, of Peter Schwartz and Peter Leyden ("The Long Boom," *Wired*, July 1997), where they point out that five streams of technology, now already in motion (personal computers, telecommunications, biotechnology, nanotechnology, and alternative energy), constitute a powerful, perhaps unavoidable, drive toward global integration.

Again, although I agree with that analysis as far as it goes, when it is seen within an all-quadrant, all-level perspective, its harsh realities are softened by the equally compelling forces *in the other quadrants*—not to mention refocused by an understanding of the archeological layers of consciousness in the interior quadrants that will *in any event* still inhabit the global techno-net (because everybody, even in a totally integral culture, is born at square one and will continue to move through that spiral, with billions of people stretching across all of the colors of the entire spectrum of consciousness).

Simply focusing on the global technological net misses a truly crucial feature: what levels of consciousness are moving through that net? What good is it if the entire globe is at moral stage 1? That would merely spell global war. Simply going "global" could mean global nightmare. There is global good and there is global bad, and unless there is a correlative consciousness development, we will have more of the latter than the former. *Unless there is Left-Hand development alongside of Right-Hand development*—unless we put as much attention on the development of consciousness as on the development of material technology—we will simply extend the reach of our collective insanity.[14] This was the conclusion also reached by UNICEF, as we saw in the last chapter, namely, that without interior development, healthy exterior development cannot be sustained.

Friedman's Lower-Right quadrant focus nonetheless helps to balance the equally lopsided picture given by analysts such as Kaplan and Huntington, who almost certainly underestimate the power of the Lower-Right quadrant (especially the emergence of system networks, the impact of cyberspace, the growth of global markets, and the diffusion of technology—all of which are reshaping the financial, environmental, and commercial domains). There is an Eros to the Kosmos: there is a subtle, slow, relentless evolutionary drift, a migratory current to unfolding events, that, in the very long run, unfolds higher and deeper connections—egocentric to ethnocentric to worldcentric. Worldcentric, globalizing technology has Eros on its side; but that does not mean that such globalization should or will carry the Western surface values with it (and there are many reasons that it should not, which is another analysis in itself). But Friedman is quite right: technology is driving a global-integral wave.

In fact, this global technological wave is basically the Lower-Right quadrant equivalent of Huntington's (Lower-Left quadrant) World Civilization. Both Huntington and Friedman are giving pieces of the puzzle as to the slow emergence of a World Civilization. As is usually the case, the techno-economic base—the LR quadrant—takes the lead first, fashioning the societies within which individuals develop. The technology usually spreads very rapidly, and then that technology slowly, over many generations, remakes the cultures arising within it. This happened with foraging, with horticultural, with agrarian, with industrial, and now it has happening with informational.

But within those techno-economic structures (agrarian, industrial, informational, etc.) in the Right Hand, there are still, in the Left Hand, the *horizontal* tectonic plates and the *vertical* memes of development—and that is where much of the action is and always will be.[15] Because, once again, *everybody* (even in a World Civilization) is born at square one and has to begin the great spiral of development from there, so that sub-pockets of culture will be a part of human civilization indefinitely (just as, within any civilization—Western, say—there are purple street gangs, red athletic tribes, blue feudal orders, green commons—and always will be, as long as human beings are born at square one). And that is why a worldcentric technology will not simply impose a homogenized culture on everybody. All of that is missed in these Lower-Right quadrant analyses that can only see surface techno-globalization.

On the other hand, an all-quadrant, all-level perspective allows us to take the best of each analysis and set them all in a larger context where their own important contributions (and limitations) can be better appreciated. All quadrants, levels, lines: The time is now ripe to move world political analysis to an integral wave.

THE WAVES OF SPIRITUAL EXPERIENCE

Let me round out this overview—which is about integrating available worldviews (or maps of the Kosmos)—with a few examples from the upper reaches of consciousness development and spiritual experiences. In various books I have presented substantial cross-cultural evidence that there are at least four different types of spiritual experiences—nature mysticism (psychic), deity mysticism (subtle), formless mysticism (causal), and nondual mysticism (nondual); and further, these are waves of increasing depth.[16] These are transpersonal and transrational waves, as contrasted with the prerational waves of magic-purple and mythic-red.[17]

The cross-cultural evidence for these higher waves is now so substantial as to put it beyond serious dispute. As only one example, Evelyn Underhill, whose *Mysticism* is justly regarded as a classic overview of Western spiritual traditions, concludes that spiritual experiences (as evidenced in the overall Western tradition) exist along a developmental continuum from *nature mysticism* (which is a type of union with the web of life) to *metaphysical mysticism* (which includes subtle illumination and formless absorption) to *divine mysticism* (and states of nondual union)—in other words, quite similar to my scheme.

This overall spectrum—from *matter* to *body* to *mind* to *soul* (psychic and subtle) to *spirit* (causal and nondual)—is, of course, nothing other than the Great Nest of Being. You can see variations on this Great Nest in figures 4-1, 4-2, and 4-3; and, indeed, as Huston Smith and numerous others have demonstrated, the cross-cultural evidence for the Great Nest is simply overwhelming.[18] Of course, I have recommended that we bring the important insights of the Great Nest into the modern world by adding quadrants and lines (as suggested in figs. 3-2, 4-5, and 5-1), thus uniting the best of ancient wisdom with the brightest of modern knowledge—and opening the way for a genuine Theory of Everything.

This recognition of a full spectrum of consciousness (such as indicated in fig. 3-2) further allows us to engage in a crucially important *cross-level* analysis, whose technical details I will reserve for an endnote,[19] but whose general point is fairly simple: a person at almost any stage of typical development (e.g., purple, red, blue, orange, green, yellow) can have an altered state of consciousness or a *peak experience* of any of the higher realms (psychic, subtle, causal, nondual). The person then *interprets* these higher experiences in the terms of the level at which the person presently resides. This calls for cross-level combinatorial analyses: for example, a person at blue can peak experience psychic, subtle, causal, nondual; so can orange, green, and so on. This gives us a grid of over two-dozen very real—and very different—types of spiritual experiences.[20]

These spiritual experiences might sound almost entirely removed from the more conventional analyses of Fukuyama, Friedman, Huntington, Kaplan, Kennedy, and crew. But, in fact, although often marginal, these religious experiences are sometimes decisive. More than one world leader, for example, in the course of the formative events in his or her life, has had a powerful peak experience or altered state, often religious in nature, that profoundly molded their subsequent worldviews and agendas, and not necessarily for the better (Hitler was a mystic of sorts, as was Rasputin). In some cases we deeply admire the results of this religious infusion (e.g., Joan of Arc, Gandhi, Martin Luther King, Jr.). In other cases we are repelled (Himmler, Charles Manson). This is where a cross-level analysis becomes crucial: what level is the spiritual experience coming from, and what level is doing the interpreting?

When egocentric levels receive a jolting infusion from the transpersonal realms, the result is usually a more empowered egocentric, often psychotic. When ethnocentric levels are hit with a transpersonal jolt, reborn furies result. When worldcentric levels are transfused, an Abraham Lincoln or a Ralph Waldo Emerson shines forth. An integral approach would make these factors an important part of an all-quadrant, all-level analysis. And not just in world leaders. Data are unreliable here, but a majority of individuals report having had at least one major spiritual or peak experience. These events are some of the most powerful motivating forces in human psychology, whether they light the face of a Mother Teresa or drive the intense fanaticism of a jihad, and no analysis of world events that ignores them can hope to succeed.

WHY DOESN'T RELIGION SIMPLY GO AWAY?

An integral analysis of the world situation immediately resolves one of the most recalcitrant problems faced by social analysts over the last two centuries: because modernity (orange) is clearly the dominant political, technological, and economic force on the face of the planet, why do all the premodern cultural movements (from purple to red to blue) still exist in overwhelming numbers? Sociologists have long predicted that modernity would simply sweep away all religious factions, since the latter are supposedly based on nothing but premodern and primitive superstition. And yet the modern world is still chock-a-bloc with various religious movements that simply refuse to go away. Why?

Answer: even in the modern world, everybody is born at wave 1 (beige), and must begin their migratory development from there, passing through purple, red, and blue on the way to orange (and green and higher). Given the pyramid of development (where the higher the level, the fewer who tend to reach it), there will always be a large population of humanity at the magic and mythic waves, which are usually associated with traditional religion. Thus, traditional religious beliefs will never completely go away because everybody is born at square one.

At the very least, policy analysts lacking a more integral overview will fail to grasp the central psychological dynamics of actual human populations. These flatland analysts consequently imagine that, for example, simply forcing orange technology or green human rights on purple, red, and blue populations will somehow solve the problem, when all it often produces is a fanatic blue jihad or a furious red revolt. A traditional "religious" orientation—purple, red, or blue—is deeply embedded in approximately 70 percent of the world's population, and thus orange and green policy analysts would do well to adopt a more integral, full-spectrum analysis that takes those stubborn facts into clear account, or their analyses will likely continue to be met with often hackneyed results.

And that refers only to narrow religion. As for deep religion (or the spirituality of the higher, post-turquoise, transpersonal waves), the frequency of those experiences will become more and more common as the center of gravity of humanity slowly drifts higher and higher. The prerational religions were dominant in the past, in premodern times, but the transrational religions are on their way, destined to descend on a collective humanity with a global consciousness at their core.

Research from individuals who are at second tier already indicates, as we saw, that at these levels there is a characteristic belief that "the earth is one organism with a collective mind." Well, that turquoise insight, research also confirms, simply *increases* at coral/psychic, where it blossoms into a genuine nature mysticism, and from there into deity, formless, and nondual deep spirituality. These higher waves do not leave behind the lower waves—somebody at the subtle still has access to orange rationality, green sensitivity, and second-tier holism—because each wave transcends and includes.

What this does mean, however, is that prerational religion will always be with us because everybody starts at square one; and transrational religions will become ever more common as humanity continues to evolve. Those who had hoped that we were rid of all that silly religious stuff are probably in for a rocky ride.

INTEGRAL PRACTICE

Allow me to repeat what was said at the beginning of this chapter. All of the theories presented in this chapter are just that: theories, or maps of the world. As such, they are a useful part of helping us attain a more integral vision. At the same time, the basic *capacity* for integral, second-tier thinking does not demand that you memorize all these different systems. You do not have to memorize the various levels, or know all of the civilization blocks, or work on making comprehensive maps yourself. However, that second-tier capacity is exercised and encouraged by engaging these integral maps, because such maps open our minds, and thus our hearts, to a more expansive, inclusive, compassionate, and integral embrace of the Kosmos and all of its inhabitants. Big pictures and big maps help open the mind, and thus the heart, to an integral transformation.

But if you have read this far, you already have the capacity for second-tier integral consciousness (or you would have stopped reading long ago). What is required is not so much to learn my particular maps as to put your own integral capacity into practice. It is to this integral practice that we can now turn.

7

One Taste

A human being is part of the whole called by us universe, a part limited in time and space. He experiences himself, his thoughts and feelings as something separated from the rest, a kind of optical delusion of his consciousness. This delusion is a kind of prison for us, restricting us to our personal desires and to affection for a few persons nearest to us. Our task must be to free ourselves from this prison by widening our circle of compassion to embrace all living creatures and the whole of nature in its beauty.

—ALBERT EINSTEIN

RIGHT AFTER I FINISHED WRITING *The Marriage of Sense and Soul*, I decided to keep a personal journal for one year. The primary reason for doing so is that most academic writing avoids any sort of personal disclosure or subjective statements, which are taken to be evidence of "biases" or "nonobjective reporting." There is some merit to that requirement, but not always, especially if the area under investigation is the subjective domain anyway. So I decided, for one year, to keep a journal that chronicled my day-to-day activities, including spiritual practice.

What I most wanted to convey in *One Taste* was some notion of an integral life, a life that finds room for body, mind, soul, and spirit as they all unfold in self, culture, and nature. In other words, it attempts to be as "all-quadrant, all-level" as one can be at any given stage. Not that I have achieved an integral life—I have never claimed that—but simply that it is an ideal worthy of aspiration. *One Taste* also gives the specific details of my version of an integral transformative practice (which I will summarize in a moment).

Most of our spirituality books are treatises on the spiritual life divorced from real life. When we read a book called *How to Know God* or *Finding Your Sacred Self*, we do not expect to see chapters on making money, having sex, drinking wine, and vacationing in Hawaii. It is therefore profoundly jarring to see genuinely spiritual accounts right in the middle of a trip to South Beach—which is exactly why I did it. Conservative fundamentalists—who believe in prescriptive morality—were alarmed that this looked suspiciously like sin; while liberals—who do not believe in interior causation, or even in interiors—were alarmed that I was devoting any attention, contemplative or otherwise, to subjective realities instead of working tirelessly for exterior economic redistribution. That both conservatives and liberals were alarmed by the book does not guarantee the book's integral truth, but it is a prerequisite.

Again, not that I have mastered this integral endeavor, but simply that I wanted a journal that did not compartmentalize—that did not set spirituality against life, but instead set spirituality in the very midst of daily work, play, parties, illness, vacations, sex, money, and family—and that invited readers to be more friendly toward an integral approach in their own lives.

Of course, there are times when it is perfectly appropriate to temporarily compartmentalize in order to focus on a specific type of development—whether that be learning to cook, going on a nature hike, or taking up a contemplative practice at a meditation retreat. For spiritual development, I have always been a strong advocate of meditation, in any of its numerous forms. Thus, the second major point I wanted to get across in *One Taste* is the importance of meditation or contemplation as part of an integral practice.

Fortunately, by far the most common feedback I received from *One Taste* was: "I started to meditate," or "After reading the book I went on an intensive meditation retreat," or "I vowed to strengthen my meditation practice." That is the single effect I hoped the book would have. Truly, adopting a new holistic philosophy, believing in Gaia, or even thinking in integral terms—however important those might be, they are the least important when it comes to spiritual transformation. Finding out *who* believes in all those things: There is the doorway to God.

INTEGRAL TRANSFORMATIVE PRACTICE

The basic idea of integral transformative practice (ITP) is simple: the more aspects of our being that we simultaneously exercise, the more likely that transformation will occur. In other words, ITP attempts to be as "all-level, all-quadrant" as possible. The more you do so, the more likely you will transform to the next higher wave. If you are at blue, this will help you transform to orange. If you are at green, this will help you move into second tier. If you are already at second tier, this will help you move into the transpersonal, spiritual waves—not merely as an altered state, but as a permanent trait.

"All-level" refers to the waves of existence, from matter to body to mind to soul to spirit; "all-quadrant" refers to the I, we, and it dimensions (or self, culture, and nature; art, morals, and science; first-person, second-person, and third-person). Thus, an "all-level, all-quadrant" practice means exercising physical, emotional, mental, and spiritual waves in self, culture, and nature.

Start with self: the waves of existence (from physical to emotional to mental to spiritual) as they appear in oneself can be exercised by a spectrum of practices: physical exercise (weightlifting, diet, jogging, yoga), emotional exercises (qi gong, counseling, psychotherapy), mental exercises (affirmation, visualization), and spiritual exercises (meditation, contemplative prayer).

But these waves of existence need to be exercised—not just in self (boomeritis!)—but in culture and nature as well. Exercising the waves in culture might mean getting involved in community service, working with the hospice movement, participating in local government, working with inner-city rehabilitation, providing services for homeless people. It can also mean using *relationships in general* (marriage, friendship, parenting) to further your own growth and the growth of others. Mutually respectful dialogue is indeed the time-honored method of linking self and other in a dance of understanding, a dance which is deeply conducive to integral embrace.

Exercising the waves of existence in nature means that nature is viewed, not as an inert and instrumental backdrop to our actions, but as participating in our own evolution. Getting actively involved in respect for nature, in any number of ways (recycling, environmental protection, nature celebration) not only honors nature, it promotes our own capacity to care.

In short, integral transformative practice attempts to exercise all of the basic waves of human beings—physical, emotional, mental, and spiritual—in self, culture, and nature. One is thus as "all-level, all-quadrant" as one can be at whatever one's actual wave of development, and this is the most powerful way to trigger transformation to the next wave—not to mention simply becoming as healthy as one can be at one's present wave, whatever it might be (no small accomplishment!).

Of course, if an individual is at, say, the blue wave, one cannot *permanently* access higher waves, including the transpersonal waves (as only one reason: the blue, ethnocentric, conventional wave is not yet at a postconventional or worldcentric stance, and thus it cannot see that Spirit shines equally in all sentient beings, and hence it cannot master global compassion, which locks it out of genuine spiritual awareness). These individuals can, however, have an altered state or a temporary peak experience of these transpersonal realms, as we saw.

What those peak experiences can do—and what meditation can do—is to help people disidentify with whatever stage they are at, and thus move to the next stage. And, in fact, we have considerable evidence that meditation does exactly that. It has been shown, for example, that meditation increases the percentage of the population who are at second tier from less than 2 percent to an astonishing 38 percent (see *The Eye of Spirit*, chap. 10). Thus, meditation is an important part of a truly integral practice.

Michael Murphy and George Leonard pioneered the first practical ITP in their book, *The Life We Are Given*. I have continued to work closely with Mike and George in elucidating the theoretical underpinnings of such a practice. There are now approximately forty ITP groups around the country (if you are interested in starting or joining such, you can contact Murphy and Leonard at www.itp-life.com). The Stanford Center for Research in Disease Prevention (of the Stanford University School of Medicine) is monitoring several groups of individuals engaged in this practice, which has already had some rather extraordinary effects, testament to what an integral transformative practice can facilitate. There are many other, similar types of all-quadrant, all-level approaches being developed around the country, and I expect to see an explosion of interest in these types of more comprehensive programs, simply because they are more effective in initiating transformation.

Recommendations

My recommendation for those who want to take up an integral transformative practice is therefore to read *One Taste* and *The Life We Are Given*; those books have all the necessary details to get started on your own ITP. I also recommend reading Robert Kegan's *In Over Our Heads* (a superb discussion of psychological transformation); Tony Schwartz, *What Really Matters—Searching for Wisdom in America* (an overview of many growth technologies that can be included in an integral practice); and Roger Walsh's *Essential Spirituality*, which I believe is the single best book on the great wisdom traditions, stressing that, at their core, they are spiritual and contemplative sciences (good science, not narrow science). For those who would like an overview of the integral approach, I recommend both *Integral Psychology* and *A Brief History of Everything*.

True but Partial

As I have continued, in several books, to elucidate suggestions for a more integral approach to various fields, I have gotten two major reactions to this work. The first, and fortunately largest, has been enthusiastic. The second has been negative and angry. A part of this anger is simply that some people resent a more integral approach; they feel that I am trying to force these ideas on them, that the holistic overview I have suggested somehow robs them of their freedom, that these ideas are a conceptual straitjacket against which they must fight.

But the real intent of my writing is not to say, you must think in this way. The real intent is to enrich: here are some of the many important facets of this extraordinary Kosmos; have you thought about including them in your own worldview? My work is an attempt to make room in the Kosmos for all of the dimensions, levels, domains, waves, memes, modes, individuals, cultures, and so on ad infinitum.

In this Theory of Everything, I have one major rule: *Everybody* is right. More specifically, everybody—including me—has some important pieces of truth, and all of those pieces need to be honored, cherished, and included in a more gracious, spacious, and compassionate embrace, a genuine T.O.E.

AND IT IS ALL UNDONE

In the end we will find, I believe, the inherent joy in existence itself, a joy that stems from the great perfection of this and every moment, a wondrous whole in itself, a part of the whole of the next, a sliding series of wholes and parts that cascade to infinity and back, never lacking and never wanting because always fulfilled in the brilliance that is now. The integral vision, having served its purpose, is finally outshined by the radiance of a Spirit that is much too obvious to see and much too close to reach, and the integral search finally succeeds by letting go of the search itself, there to dissolve in a radical Freedom and consummate Fullness that was always already the case, so that one abandons a theory of everything in order simply to be Everything, one with the All in this endless awareness that holds the Kosmos kindly in its hand. And then the true Mystery yields itself, the face of Spirit secretly smiles, the Sun rises in your very own heart and the Earth becomes your very own body, galaxies rush through your veins while the stars light up the neurons of your night, and never again will you search for a mere theory of that which is actually your own Original Face.

Notes

CHAPTER 1: THE AMAZING SPIRAL

1. This more comprehensive view of the Kosmos, this T.O.E., can include strings and membranes, but is not reducible to them. Those who have read *Sex, Ecology, Spirituality* (SES) will recognize that string theory (or M-theory) is perfectly compatible with the twenty tenets (or the basic patterns demonstrated by all holons in all domains). According to SES, reality is fundamentally composed—not of particles, quarks, pointless dimensions, strings, or membranes—but of *holons*. A holon is a whole that is simultaneously a part of other wholes. For example, a whole quark is part of a whole proton; a whole proton is part of a whole atom; a whole atom is part of a whole molecule; a whole molecule is part of a whole cell, which is a part of a whole organism, which is part of the whole Kosmos, which is part of the whole of the Kosmos of the next moment, and so ad infinitum (what SES calls "turtles all the way up, all the way down"). What *all* of those entities are, before they are anything else, are holons—they are all whole/parts. The Kosmos is made of holons at various levels of organization (physical holons, emotional holons, mental holons, spiritual holons). This insight relieves us from saying that, for example, the entire Kosmos is made of nothing but quarks, which is horribly reductionistic. Rather, each higher level of holons has emergent qualities that cannot be derived from, nor totally reduced to, its junior levels—and this gives us the Kosmos, not merely the cosmos.

The lower the level of organization of a holon, the more *fundamental* it is; the higher the level, the more *significant* it is. Thus, a quark is a very fundamental holon, because it is a part of so many other wholes (it is a subholon in atoms, molecules, cells, etc.). A cell, on the other hand, is more significant, because, being higher on the organizational scale, it contains so many other holons *within its own makeup* (it contains, or signifies, molecules and atoms and quarks). Thus, the lower holons are more fundamental, the higher holons are more significant. The lower holons are necessary, but not sufficient, ingredients of the higher holons, which in turn give meaning and significance to the lower holons. The higher holons *contain more being* because they contain so many other holons within their own makeup.

As explained in SES, there is ample evidence that there are no upper limits to holons ("turtles all the way up"). The question is, are there any lower limits? That is, are there any truly *fundamental* holons (which would be, by definition, parts of other wholes, but containing no parts themselves)? Is it turtles all the way down, too, or do we run into fundamental holons that cannot be further divided?

My position in SES is that it is, and always will be, turtles all the way up *and* down—that every time we find what we think are the most fundamental units or holons, they are eventually found to contain even more fundamental holons. I suggested that, in fact, each time human consciousness evolves to a higher and more powerful level, it will discover deeper and more fundamental holons, and this is basically unending.

Well, string theory is just another version of that never-ending story. For a long time it was thought that protons, neutrons, and electrons were as fundamental as you could get. Then came the standard model, and those holons were found to be composed of smaller holons, namely, various types of quarks, existing alongside a whole panoply of muons, gluons, bosons, neutrinos, and other assorted holons. These, the standard model proclaimed, are actually the rock-bottom fundamental units (modeled in dimensionless-point mathematics).

String theory upset all of that. Starting in the 1980s, it was suggested that quarks—and, indeed, all physical forces, particles, and antiparticles—were produced by resonating patterns of fundamental entities called *strings*. Unlike the standard model of physics, which postulates dimensionless points as the fundamental units of existence, strings are microscopic one-dimensional lines, often looped like a rubber band. The various "notes" that these vibrating strings play actually give rise to the various particles and forces in the physical world. A more fundamental level of holons had been found.

There were several immediate advantages to string theory. Among them was the fact that giving strings an actual size reduced the theoretical quantum foam and allowed—for the first time ever—a seamless suggestion as to how quantum mechanics and relativity theory could be united. Further, one of the resonating patterns of string theory produced gravitons, and thus—also for the first time ever—gravity could be included in the new model (the old or standard model could account for electromagnetic, strong and weak nuclear, but not gravity)—hence, string theory was a theory of "everything" (meaning "everything in the physical realm").

Strings, then, were proclaimed the most fundamental holons, beneath which there was no beneath. Until the mid-1990s, when the "second revolution" in string theory, ushered in by Edward Witten (and called M-theory), suggested that strings were actually the tip of an iceberg that contained three-dimensional membranes, four-dimensional membranes, . . . up to nine-dimensional membranes (plus the tenth dimension of time), referred to altogether as "p-branes." These even more fundamental holons exist in a heterarchy of convertible forms, depending upon factors such as coupling constants, and out of this heterarchy of fundamental holons the hierarchy of higher holons emerges (strings, then quarks, then atoms, etc., as the holarchy of the Kosmos evolves). Well, all of this is familiar enough from the twenty tenets of SES, and string theory and M-theory are simply variations on these already quite familiar patterns displayed in so many other domains.

So, are the p-branes the most fundamental holons? It looks like it. That is, for the time being, until consciousness grows even stronger and thus probes the subquantum realm even more deeply, where yet more fundamental holons will wink out at us, turtles all the way down. . . .

(In principle there is nothing wrong with finding genuinely fundamental holons—that is, holons that are not decomposable into smaller holons. Many emergent lines of development start with original holon building blocks. Sentences have words which have letters, but letters are not composed of any other symbols; there the linguistic symbol line begins. But the Kosmos *as a whole* seems to have no bottom and no top. . . .)

This present book is probably the best introduction to my work on the whole (although it can be supplemented with *A Brief History of Everything*, *Integral Psychology*, and *One Taste*). The main text for this T.O.E. remains the second revised edition of *Sex, Ecology, Spirituality*, which is out both in paperback and as volume 6 of the *Collected Works* (CW6).

2. From an overemphasis on the social construction of reality (the omnipotent cultural self creates all realities), to the relativity of knowledge (all knowledge is culturally relative, except my own omniscient knowledge that this is so), to extreme deconstruction (I have the power to explode all texts), to reader-response theory (when I view an artwork it is actually I, not the artist, who creates the artwork), to theories that will resurrect and save Gaia, Goddess, and Spirit (whereas it is usually thought that Spirit will save us, not the other way around), to the new-age notion that you create your own reality (actually, psychotics create their own reality), to UFO abductions (an extraordinarily advanced intelligence wants nothing more than to look at me), to hundreds of new paradigm claims (I have the new paradigm which will transform the world). In an enormous number of different areas, this is an awful lot of power ascribed to the finite self, don't you think? Social critics who have perceived a considerable amount of "self-inflation" here are on to something important, it seems.

3. F. Richards and M. Commons in Alexander et al., *Higher Stages of Human Development*, p. 160, emphasis in original.

4. C. Graves, "Summary Statement: The Emergent, Cyclical, Double-Helix Model of the Adult Human Biopsychosocial Systems," Boston, May 20, 1981.

5. See *Integral Psychology* for extensive references to the cross-cultural research supporting the validity of these models.

6. Don Beck, personal communication; much of this data is on computer file in the National Values Center, Denton, Texas, and is open to qualified researchers.

In my own system, there are actually numerous different modules, streams, or lines proceeding relatively independently through the basic levels or waves. Individuals can be at a relatively high level of development in some modules, medium in others, and low in still others—there is nothing linear about overall development. The Graves model is what I call a "wilber-2" type of model: there is one major developmental axis, and individuals can fluctuate up and down that axis in different situations. A "wilber-3" type of model, on the other hand, maintains that, in one and the same situation, an individual can be at a high level of development in some lines, medium in others, low in still others. (A "wilber-4" model takes that model and sets it in the context of the four quadrants. See *The Eye of Spirit* [CW7] for an explanation of these four types of models.) Further, an individual can have an *altered state* or a *peak experience* at virtually any stage of development, so the notion that spiritual experiences are available only at the higher stages is incorrect (see *Integral Psychology* for a full discussion of these topics). Spiral Dynamics does not include states of consciousness, nor does it cover the higher, transpersonal waves of consciousness (see also note 10). But for the ground it covers, it gives one very useful and elegant model of the self and its journey through what Clare Graves called the "waves of existence."

Don Beck has taken steps to make the Graves model a "wilber-4" type of model; he uses the four quadrants, and he now calls his model "4Q/8L" (eight levels in all four quadrants). He is very sympathetic with the existence of transpersonal states and structures. The stages outlined in Spiral Dynamics are based on research and data, and the problem, as always, is that although altered states are very common, higher permanent stages are relatively rare (greater depth, less span). If around 0.1 percent of the population is at turquoise (as will be explained in the text), you can imagine how few are stably at even higher waves of consciousness, not as a passing state, but as an enduring trait or permanent realization. For that reason, it is very hard to get much data on any sort of genuinely higher stages, which is one of the reasons that agreement as to transpersonal waves tapers off. In one publication, Beck and Cowan give the name "coral" to the stage beyond turquoise, and then they state: "Coral, for these authors, is still unclear." Coral, in my opinion, is the psychic wave; but you can see how difficult it is getting decent data in this regard. See *Integral Psychology* for more details.

7. In this chapter we are giving only a brief outline of *structures* and *stages* (memes). In chapter 3 we will add *states*, *streams*, and *types*.

8. All of the interpretations and uses of Spiral Dynamics presented in this book have been carefully checked with Don Beck. For my friend Chris Cowan's uses and interpretations, please see cowan@spiraldynamics.com. Beck and Cowan are now working on a second revised edition of *Spiral Dynamics*, which reflects some of their more recent work. For another very interesting developmental model inspired by Graves, see Jenny Wade's *Changes of Mind*.

9. I personally believe that the numerous theories of "memes"—all of which basically maintain that memes are the units of a type of natural selection process operating in the mental and cultural realms, transmitted similarly to a virus of the mind, with survival (as functional fit) again the rule—are

deeply confused theories. My objections are numerous. As the term is generally used, (1) memes are units that are explained in third-person it-language, so they fail to capture the Left-Hand or interior quadrants of I and we; (2) as such, memes are classic examples of subtle reductionism, and the use of the term hurts more than helps an integral cause, because once you have reduced consciousness to it-units, there is little to prevent scientific materialism and gross reductionism; (3) memes as typically pictured are individual mental-cultural units, and thus the theory of memes fails to grasp that every unit in existence (other than heaps or aggregates) is a holon, a compound individual with a specific development enfolded in it, so that each meme actually is composed of subholons linked by a vertical developmental archeology and not merely a horizontal history; (4) thus, memes are simply the units of the mind and culture as conceived by flatland (that is, memes are distorted and inaccurate two-dimensional pictures of four-dimensional holons: they are pictured as one-dimensional viruses that move forward in a second dimension of time, selected for survival by the sole criteria of functional fit; whereas in reality they are at least three-dimensional holons—i.e., they possess the dimensions of I, we, and it, or an interior (I), an exterior (it), and a shared interior (we)—moving through the fourth dimension of time, and selected for survival according to the validity criteria of all three dimensions (the Big Three validity claims, or, more accurately, the validity claims of all four quadrants [for a fuller discussion of "dimensions," see later in this note]); (5) even within flatland, the vast majority of scientists reject the concept of memes because of its lack of operational specifications.

Nonetheless, a few people use "meme" in a more adequate, four-quadrant fashion. Don Beck is one, and because we are presenting Spiral Dynamics, I must use the terminology of memes. In some ways this is unfortunate, because when the theory of memes ceases to be the intellectual fad that it is, it will likely take down all those theories associated with it. This is why I will continually emphasize that the research strongly supports the notion of stages or waves of consciousness development, and "memes" is just a particular, somewhat less-than-happy way to frame this research. Beck is very careful about this, and I am comfortable with his formulations; but he is a rare exception. Whenever I use the term "meme," I specifically mean a mental-cultural quadratic holon, as explained above.

As for "dimensions," the word has numerous meanings, and thus it is very difficult, without lengthy explanation (as in the following), to be consistent. In physics, there are generally thought to be four dimensions in the macro world: three spatial dimensions (length, height, width) and the dimension of time: thus, four dimensions of physical spacetime. In string and M-theory, however, the physical domain is said to consist of nine or ten microspatial dimensions, plus the dimension of time, for a total of around ten or eleven dimensions.

But all of those dimensions cover *only* the physical realm. In the worldview of scientific materialism, that is all the realms there are. But if we acknowledge that there are emotional, mental, and spiritual dimensions to existence, then we start running into terminology problems, because there are only so many words to go around.

Most often, as explained in *The Marriage of Sense and Soul* (CW8), I use *levels* and *dimensions* in this fashion: levels refers to *vertical* structures or waves, and dimensions refers to *horizontal* aspects found at the levels. The most prominent dimensions, found at each level, are simply the four quadrants (I, we, it, and its; or subjective, intersubjective, objective, and interobjective "spaces"). Since both "it" and "its" are objective dimensions, I often condense these four dimensions to the Big Three (of I, we, and it; or art, morals, and science; or the Beautiful, the Good, and the True; and so on).

Thus, in this terminology, each level of being has at least these four dimensions. If there are, say, five major levels of being (matter, body, mind, soul, and spirit), each of which has four dimensions or four quadrants, then there are twenty level-dimensions of being (e.g., a physical I, an emotional I, a mental I, a soul-I, and a spirit-I; plus a physical we, an emotional we, a mental we, and so on. . . .).

Each level has a different type or experience of time. For example, there is physical time (as measured by a clock); emotional time (which is how this moment feels to you as it unfolds); mental time (which is the time in which history unfolds: when you think about your life, it unfolds in narrative time, the time of stories and myths and dramas and plays—a genuinely real time, the time of the symbolic narrative); and spiritual time (in which eternity can be seen in the timeless moment). All of those are real levels of time, or the ways in which the Kosmos unfolds at different levels of being. (See *The Atman Project* and *Up from Eden* for a discussion of the many levels of time; both of those books are contained in CW2.)

It is common to count time as another (though inseparable) dimension. If we do so, this means that each level has at least five dimensions (namely, the four quadrants as they each unfold in that level's time). With five major levels, each of which has four "spatial" dimensions (I, we, it, and its) and a correlative time dimension, then we have twenty-five level-dimensions of being.

The physical it-dimension, which is said to contain 9 or 10 microphysical dimensions, I count as merely one dimension (while not denying its 9 or 10 subdimensions). The physical plane also contains a rudimentary I, we, and its dimension. But you can see how dizzying this whole affair of dimensions can become!

As I said, without these lengthy types of definitions, it is hard to be consistent with a term like "dimensions," and thus sometimes, for convenience, I use the term in my technical sense as being equivalent to "quadrants" (or to any horizontal aspects of any of the levels), and sometimes I use the term loosely to mean either vertical levels or horizontal dimensions. The context should make it clear which is meant.

10. Personal communication. Beck uses meme in a specific sense, which he calls a "value meme" or vMEME, which is defined as "a core value system, a worldview, an organizing principle that permeates thought structures, decision-making systems, and various expressions of culture."

The Graves/Beck system does not clearly distinguish between transitional and enduring structures, nor between basic and self-related structures. In my own system, the basic structures are enduring and remain fully active capacities available at all later stages, but most of the self-related streams (such as morals, values, and self-identity) consist of transitional stages which tend to be replaced by subsequent stages. (Subpersonalities can exist at different levels or memes, however, so that one can indeed have a purple subpersonality, a blue subpersonality, and so on. These often are context-triggered, so that one can have quite different types of moral responses, affects, needs, etc., in different situations.) But in general, for the central or proximate self, once its *center of gravity* reaches, say, green, it will not activate a pure purple meme unless it is regressing; but it can (and constantly does) *activate the corresponding basic structures* of the purple meme (namely, the emotional-phantasmic level). When a green adult "activates" a purple meme, that is not the identical meme the 2-year-old child possesses. For the 2-year-old, the purple meme is the basis of the infant's central identity, its *proximate self* (or "I"), whereas for a green adult, it is part of the *distal self* (or "me"). When the green adult "activates purple," he or she is actually activating the basic capacities (basic structures) first laid down during the "purple period" (e.g., phantasmic-emotional), but because the self's exclusive identity is no longer at the purple level, the corresponding transitional structures (morals, values, worldviews) are not fully activated unless one is regressing (or unless one is activating a purple subpersonality). So, at the least, I would differentiate between "purple capacities" and "purple self"; the former are enduring, the latter is transitional. See *Integral Psychology* for a further discussion of these issues; see also note 6.

Still, these are technical distinctions, about which there is much room for friendly disagreement; and the Graves/Beck system, in speaking of "activating memes," offers a simple and concise way to deal with the most general and important facets of these waves of existence (such as the fact that there are indeed general waves of consciousness, but once they emerge, you can activate any of them under various circumstances, so that you can indeed be a "different person" in different situations, and so on). I also find that, especially for educational purposes, the more technical distinctions (enduring/transitional, basic/self) confuse more than edify, and a generalized discussion of memes more than suffices to help people think in terms of the entire spiral of development, the entire spectrum of consciousness. For the simple and crucial point is that all of us have all of these waves of consciousness available to us as potentials that can unfold under facilitating circumstances.

11. Much of the following descriptions consist of direct quotes or paraphrasing

from various publications of Graves, Beck, and Beck and Cowan. See *Integral Psychology* for references.

12. See note 6.

13. This "union of feeling and knowledge" is one of the general definitions of the mature centaur (see *Brief History*). In my model, and referring for the moment just to the cognitive line, green is early vision-logic (and the transition from formop to vision-logic). As such, green or early vision-logic differentiates formal systems into multiple contexts. Middle and late vision-logic (yellow and turquoise) then integrate those differentiations to varying degrees (while introducing their own, new differentiations that later waves will integrate). Coral is psychic, the beginning of truly transpersonal waves. See *Integral Psychology* for a full elaboration of these topics.

14. All of the positive items mentioned in this paragraph actually begin with the orange meme (and historically, with the Enlightenment), because orange, as we will see, is the first truly worldcentric, postconventional wave of development. Green is simply an intensification and expansion of worldcentric fairness; its attacks on orange are largely misguided and often driven by an intense form of boomeritis (see chap. 2; see also *Boomeritis*).

15. See *One Taste*, November 23 entry, for references and extended discussion.

CHAPTER 2: BOOMERITIS

1. This is not to deny the existence of various sorts of infant and childhood spirituality, only that the vehicles through which they are expressed are largely preconventional and egocentric. See *Integral Psychology*, chap. 11, "Is There a Childhood Spirituality?"

2. *The Quest for Mind*, p. 63.

3. See note 1.

4. See H. Haan et al., "Moral Reasoning of Young Adults," *Journal of Personality and Social Psychology*, 1968, 10, pp. 183-201.

5. As indicated in note 12 for chap. 1, worldcentric and egalitarian fairness begins with orange (and the Enlightenment), which deserves most of the difficult credit, but reaches something of a zenith with green, which historically extended legal, political, and civil rights to even more groups of people that were previously marginalized, not by orange, but by blue and red (a fact consistently overlooked by green's misguided and totalizing attacks on the Enlightenment. See *Boomeritis* for an extensive discussion of this theme).

6. Actualization hierarchies I also refer to as *holarchies*, which will be explained in chap. 3. Students of my work will notice that in that series (atoms to molecules . . . to universe), I am not differentiating individual (upper quadrants) and collective (lower quadrants). In actuality, individual and collective are correlative aspects of all holons at every level of development (see SES). But for the simple example given in the text, the conclusion remains the same.

7. Jenny Wade, who has made a careful study of Graves, believes that orange (achievement) and green (affiliative) are not two different levels but two different choices offered to blue (conformist), so that both orange and green can advance directly to second tier (authentic). Wade's book, *Changes of Mind*, is a superb overview of the spectrum of consciousness; it is discussed at length in the second edition of *The Eye of Spirit* (CW7).

8. See *One Taste*, September 23 entry, for a discussion of Ray's integral culture as an example of the newly emerging Person-Centered Civil Religion.

9. Don Beck, personal communication. Notice that in the description of the green meme in chapter 1, Beck and Cowan estimate that around 10 percent of the world's population is at green, but most of that is in America and Europe. Beck's research indicates that around 20 percent of adult Americans are green meme, a close match to Ray's figures.

10. See *The Eye of Spirit* (CW7) for references and discussion of these data; see also *Integral Psychology* for an overview.

CHAPTER 3: AN INTEGRAL VISION

1. What follows is a four-quadrant analysis of the change factors necessary for personal transformation. Since I have not yet introduced or defined the quadrants, I am not naming them. But students of my work will immediately recognize them.

2. Of course, by "break down," Graves means that the *fixation* to green has to be transcended. The green meme itself remains a crucial component in the overall Spiral.

3. The quote is from Michael Murphy, cofounder of Esalen Institute, author of *The Future of the Body* and *Golf in the Kingdom*. See the Foreword to *The Eye of Spirit* (CW7).

4. The books following SES all flesh out its various ideas; these books include *A Brief History of Everything*, *The Eye of Spirit*, *The Marriage of Sense and Soul*, *One Taste*, and *Integral Psychology*. For a popular introduction, I recommend *A Brief History of Everything*.

5. Don Beck has also begun using a figure similar to this, which he calls "4Q/8L" to refer to eight levels in all four quadrants. Of course, I extend the levels to include the higher, transpersonal waves and states, and I include numerous different altered states and developmental streams progressing through the major waves, but this simplified figure is quite adequate to make our general points. Incidentally, if you would like to work with Don Beck in applying this "graves/wilber" model and Spiral Dynamics in general, you can contact him at spiwiz@iglobal.net. See also the work of Peter McNab, Wyatt Woodsmall, Brian van der Horst, and Maureen Silos, among others.

6. Evidence for these independent modules is presented in *The Eye of Spirit* (CW7) and *Integral Psychology*.

7. Technically, the Gravesian values are a line of development; but the levels in that line—which, in my system, are actually levels of consciousness—can be used to represent levels in general. See *Integral Psychology*.

8. There are many different meanings of the words "integrated" or "integral" as they apply to a stage of human development.

To begin with, there are at least two different general meanings: horizontal and vertical. Horizontal integration means that the elements of any given level—purple, blue, yellow, etc.—are fairly well integrated *at that level*. A well-integrated level is a healthy level, or the very best that that level can be given its inherent structures and limitations. Horizontal integration basically involves *an integration of the four quadrants at any given level*. Conversely, an imbalance (or lack of integration) of the four quadrants at any level (e.g., an overemphasis on the I, we, or it domains) results in a pathological imbalance at that level. Restoring health at that level means restoring a balance or integration of the elements and quadrants at that level (e.g., moving from unhealthy blue to healthy blue). Such is horizontal integration.

Vertical integration, on the other hand, means moving to a higher level of integration altogether. Now, at this point, definitions of "integral" begin to diverge sharply, depending upon the highest level of development recognized by a particular theorist. The fact is, each level of development has the capacity to be relatively *more integrative* than its predecessors, simply because each healthy level "transcends and includes," and thus each senior level can embrace more holons in its own being and thus is relatively *more integral*.

Thus, various theorists tend to call the highest level that they recognize "integral." For example, Gebser's levels are archaic, magic, mythic, rational, and integral. Jane Loevinger's levels include autistic, symbiotic, impulsive, safety, conformist, conscientious, individualistic, autonomous, and integrated. Spiral Dynamics refers to its highest levels (second tier) with terms like integral and holistic, and so on.

You can see most of those terms in fig. 2-1, which covers levels of consciousness up to what I call the "centaur." But notice that I believe there are even higher levels or waves, which I have indicated as "transpersonal" (or "third tier"). In numerous books I have traced these higher levels of consciousness using extensive cross-cultural research (see *Integral Psychology*). We could very well call the highest of those waves "integral," since they are even more integrated than the centaur, Gebser's integral-aperspectival, Loevinger's integrated, and so on. The point, again, is simply that each developmental wave is relatively more integral than its predecessors, and thus what we call "the" integral level depends upon the highest level that we recognize.

Because the highest level that most researchers recognize is centauric (integral-aperspectival, second tier, etc.), I have throughout this book generally used the term "integral" to refer to those levels. But it should be understood that this is actually a very relative term, and that the ultimate integral level is the nondual Kosmos itself, which is simultaneously the highest level of your own consciousness and the Ground of each and every level without exception.

9. This can occur in any of the lines. For example, in the moral line, a person might be predominantly enneagram type 7 at the green wave in the context of the workplace; under stress, the person might move to type 1 at the orange wave (or even blue wave); cognitively, the person might be type 4 at turquoise, and so on. Notice, however, that what the enneagram alone cannot spot is the shift in vertical levels. An orange 7 under stress might go to orange 1, as enneagram theory maintains; but under real stress, orange 7 will regress to blue, then red or purple. These are not just different types, but different levels of types. Again, by combining horizontal typologies with vertical typologies, we can make use of second-tier constructions for a more integral view.

I first suggested using horizontal typologies, such as the enneagram, with the vertical levels of development in *A Brief History of Everything*. Other researchers have independently arrived at similar suggestions. Incidentally, some versions of the enneagram are used in a vertical fashion, as *levels* of development (gut to heart to crown) and not as types available at every level. That is fine, too; I have used the latter version since that is now the most popular.

10. For a good summary of Gilligan's hierarchical view of male and female development, see Alexander and Langer, *Higher Stages of Human Development*, especially the editors' Introduction and Gilligan's chap. 9.

11. The conclusion in *The Eye of Spirit* is that men tend to translate with emphasis on agency, women on communion; and men tend to transform with an emphasis on Eros, women on Agape. But the general waves of development remain essentially same in both sexes; in themselves, they are gender neutral. See chap. 8 of *The Eye of Spirit* (CW7), "Integral Feminism."

12. Thus, using our example of Spiral Dynamics, females would develop through the same waves of existence (or the developmental hierarchy) as males, but with a more relational, permeable, or communal orientation, and an integral feminism would dedicate itself to exploring the dynamics and patterns in all of the waves, states, and streams, as they appear in this "different voice." See *The Eye of Spirit* (CW7), chap. 8, "Integral Feminism."

13. See *Integral Psychology* for a full discussion of the topic of structures and states.

14. For the unwarranted nature of the reduction of the Upper-Left quadrant to the Upper Right, see *Integral Psychology* and *A Brief History of Everything*. The exact relation of mind and brain is explored in detail in *Integral Psychology*.

15. This does not mean that systems sciences apply only to the Lower-Right quadrant; increasingly the Upper-Right quadrant—especially brain mechanisms—are also approached in systems terms. It is simply that the UR is an individual holon, and the LR is a social holon. But both have systems

aspects, because all individuals are actually compound individuals. See SES for a discussion of this theme.

But notice: systems theory covers only the Right-Hand quadrants (whether Upper or Lower). *This is why systems theory (and chaos and complexity theories) cannot adequately model consciousness (or the interior quadrants).* As Whitehead, Hartshorne, and David Ray Griffin have pointed out, the only holons that possess consciousness are individual holons. That is, only compound individuals possess consciousness. Collectives or societies do not possess consciousness themselves (although they possess compound individuals, which do possess consciousness). Put simply, all varieties of systems theory are structured in "it" language, whereas consciousness is structured in "I" language. The many approaches to modeling consciousness in systems theory terms (chaos, complexity, autopoiesis) are thus considerably off the mark.

This is not to say that they are without importance. In my model, the Lower-Right quadrant is an important part of the overall story of consciousness, since all holons contain four quadrants. Systems approaches are important for giving that aspect of consciousness that involves its exterior forms in collective systems. But the systems approaches need to be supplemented with "I" and "we" models and methods. See "An Integral Theory of Consciousness," CW7.

16. Technically, "we" is first-person plural, and "you" is second person. But I include first-person plural ("we") and second person ("you/Thou") as both being in the Lower-Left quadrant, which I refer to in general as "we." The reason I do so is that there is no second-person plural in English (which is why Southerners have to say "you all" and Northerners say "you guys"). In other words, when "we" is being done with respect, it implicitly includes an I-Thou relationship (I cannot truly understand thee unless WE share a set of common perceptions).

So in my opinion the I-Thou theorists are all doing a subset of Lower-Left quadrant, or "we" in the broadest sense. And that is certainly how most "we" theorists, such as Habermas, also view the intersubjective realm (namely, true I-Thou is a subset of We). Otherwise, second-person "you" can degenerate into seeing you as an object or "it." Thus, all true second-person research is implicitly first-person plural, or intersubjective we (at least in part, even as the Thou is differentiated from the We). Thus, merely emphasizing "I-Thou" or second-person research can in itself be objectifying and demeaning. In any event, I have been a strong advocate of we/Thou, intersubjective research, as have most of the great hermeneutic philosophers. And I very much agree that this intersubjective domain (in both we and Thou) has been horribly neglected by it-science and I-subjectivism. An "all-quadrant, all-level" approach—or a 1-2-3 approach—makes ample room for I, we, and it research.

17. As for the relation between states of consciousness and structures of consciousness, see *Integral Psychology*.

18. See *Integral Psychology* for a discussion of the self, the levels of pathology, and the typical treatment modalities.

CHAPTER 4: SCIENCE AND RELIGION

1. See especially *Eye to Eye* (CW2), *The Marriage of Sense and Soul* (CW8), and *Integral Psychology*.
2. Ian G. Barbour, *Religion and Science—Historical and Contemporary Issues*.
3. Eugenie Scott, "The 'Science and Religion Movement,'" *Skeptical Inquirer*, July/August 1999.
4. For the importance of constructive postmodernism, see *The Marriage of Sense and Soul* (CW8), *Integral Psychology*, and *Boomeritis*.
5. In Barbour's central text on this topic, *Religion and Science—Historical and Contemporary Issues*, he points out that the data of religion involve spiritual experiences. "The data for a religious community consist of the distinctive experiences of individuals and the stories and rituals of a religious tradition." Unlike critics who imagine that recourse to the word "data" implies some sort of positivism, Barbour realizes that "data" means any raw material from any realm, and this includes mystical experiences. But Barbour then devotes less than two pages (out of an almost 400-page book) to actually discussing this data—what it is, how it is gotten, how it is verified or rejected, and so on. This large vacuum is typical of the approaches that I summarized in the main text, a vacuum that *The Marriage of Sense and Soul* attempts to fill. I will later outline why and how data fit into good science (including the parts of spiritual experience that are open to investigation by good science).

   I find much of what Barbour does say to be insightful and useful, and I am in agreement with a good deal of it as far as it goes; but in slighting the actual nature of the data of religion, he falls short of the heart of the matter, in my opinion.
6. S. Gould, "Non-Overlapping Magisteria," *Skeptical Inquirer*, July/August 1999. His italics.
7. S. Gould, "Non-Overlapping Magisteria," *Skeptical Inquirer*, July/August 1999; my italics.
8. For my strong criticisms of the perennial philosophy and the traditional Great Chain, see note 16.
9. See Wilber, *The Eye of Spirit*, and Alexander and Langer, *Higher Stages of Human Development*.
10. In the Upper-Left quadrant, "rules" refers to concrete operational thinking (roughly, blue); "formal" to formal operational thinking (roughly, orange); and "vision-logic" to systems thinking (green, yellow, and turquoise). In the Upper-Right quadrant, SF1, SF2, and SF3 refer to "structure-functions" of the brain that are the correlates of rules, formal, and vision-logic. In the

Lower-Left quadrant, "uroboric" refers to the worldview of the reptilian brain stem and "typhonic" to that of the limbic system. See SES for details.

11. Such as *Sex, Ecology, Spirituality* (CW6); *A Brief History of Everything* (CW7); and *Integral Psychology*.

12. It is common to distinguish between "religion" (authoritarian and institutional forms) and "spirituality" (personal beliefs and experiences). In some ways that is a useful distinction, but in many ways it obscures. There are very profound personal/mystical branches of most forms of institutional religions; in fact, in many ways religion is just institutionalized spirituality (e.g., if New-Age spirituality became influential and established, it would eventually be a religion). I prefer to speak instead of narrow and broad conceptions of religion/spirituality (or shallow and deep, depending on the metaphor). This is explained further in the text. My argument applies to both "religion" and "spirituality."

13. In *A Sociable God* (CW3), I called this the difference between *legitimate* religion and *authentic* religion, the former offering effective translation (or change in surface structures), the latter offering effective transformation (or change in deep structures). The former is moving furniture around on one floor, the latter is changing floors.

14. See *Eye to Eye* (CW3), chap. 2. As for whether or not there are "immediate" experiences or only "mediated" experiences: Even if experiences—sensory, mental, or spiritual—are mediated by cultural factors (and they are, given that all holons have four quadrants), nonetheless at the time of the apprehension, the experience is immediate. That is what I mean by immediate experience or data. (See SES for extensive discussion of this theme.)

Whenever I outline these three factors (injunction, illumination, validation), I always emphasize that the paradigm or injunction *brings forth* data, it does not just *disclose* data. This is in keeping with various post-Kantian and postmodern positions that deny the "myth of the given." It is also in line with Varela's enactive paradigm. At the same time, as discussed in *Sense and Soul*, denying the myth of the given, in any domain, is not to deny certain objectively real or intrinsic features of domains. The idea that there are pure objects unaffected by perception and the idea that all realities are socially constructed are both lopsided, unsatisfactory notions. A four-quadrant epistemology steers between mere objectivism and mere subjectivism by finding room for an inherent balance of those partial truths. At the same time, due to the prevalence of extreme constructivist epistemologies, I often emphasize the objectively real components of many forms of knowing, since that is the partial but important truth that is most often being unfortunately denied. See John Searle, *The Construction of Social Reality* (i.e., as opposed to the social construction of reality), the Introduction to *The Eye of Spirit* (CW7), and *Boomeritis*.

15. But science—broad or narrow—is not, as I said, the whole story of deep spirituality. The broad science of the interior domains only gives us the immediate data or immediate experiences of those interior domains. Those

experiences are the ingredients for further elaboration in aesthetic/expressive and ethical/normative judgments. Thus, even with broad science, we are not reducing the interiors to merely science (broad or narrow). Science, in both its broad and narrow forms, is always merely one of the Big Three, and simply helps us investigate the immediate data or experiences that are the raw material of aesthetic and normative experiences. Charges that my approach is positivistic missed this point.

Thus, in *Sense and Soul,* I do indeed try to show that there is a *science* of the body realm (gross), the subtle realm (subtle), and the causal realm (spirit). But I point out that there is also the *art* of the body realm, the subtle realm, and spirit; and there are the *morals* of the body realm, the mind, and spirit. Thus, *all* of the manifest levels of the Great Nest have an I, we, and it dimension—that is, all of the levels actually have art, morals, and science. Hence, even if we expand science into the higher realms, as I suggest, science and its methods are still only "one third" of the total story, because the higher levels also have art and morals, which follow their own quite different methodologies (following their different validity claims, namely, truthfulness and justness, respectively).

Therefore, two points should be kept in mind: I have indeed suggested that we can legitimately expand science to investigate aspects not only of the body or sensorimotor realm (narrow empiricism), but also of the mind and spirit realm (the geist sciences). But even then, there are not only the sciences of the higher realms, there are the art and morals of the higher realms as well (or, more precisely, there are all four quadrants of the higher waves, each of which has a different methodology and validity claim: truth, truthfulness, justness, and functional fit).

Thus, even with an expanded definition of science, I never reduce the higher realms to science only, for there are the art and morals and science of the higher realms. And the art and morals have different specific methodologies than the sciences, as I clearly explain. A few critics proclaimed that in expanding science to include the higher realms, I was somehow reducing the higher realms to science.

Notice also that in the text I am focusing on just an individual. Broad science can also be part of the investigation of the Lower-Left quadrant and its realities. But in all of the *interior* domains, broad science is *dialogical* (and *translogical*), not merely monological: here we are in the presence of the broad sciences of phenomenology, qualitative research methodology, interpretive sciences, and so on. Narrow science, on the other hand, whether individual (e.g., physics, chemistry, biology) or collective (systems theory, chaos and complexity theories) is essentially monological: it investigates "its," not "I's" and "we's" in their own nonreductionistic terms. See *Eye to Eye* (CW3), chaps. 1 and 2; *The Eye of Spirit* (CW7); and numerous endnotes in SES (CW6).

16. Page 204.

A few critics attacked *Sense and Soul* because they identified it with the "perennial philosophy," the idea of which they rather loathe. The pluralistic relativists and the spiritual approaches based heavily on the green meme (see the Introduction to CW7) have for the past three decades aggressively attacked the very notion of a perennial philosophy. They tend to claim that there are no universal truths (except their own pluralistic ideas, which are universally true for all cultures), and they claim that the perennial philosophy, even if it does exist, is rigid and authoritarian (whereupon they often replace it with their own authoritarian, politically correct ideology). Nonetheless, I sympathize with many of the criticisms of the perennial philosophy. My extensive criticisms of the perennial philosophy can be found in *The Eye of Spirit* (CW7), *The Marriage of Sense and Soul* (CW8), *Integral Psychology* (CW4), *One Taste* (CW8), SES (CW6), and the Introductions to CW2, CW3, and CW4.

When critics identify me with the perennial philosophy, they fail to notice that the only item of the perennial philosophy that I have actually defended is the notion of realms of being and knowing, and then I only staunchly defend three of them: matter, mind, and spirit (or gross, subtle, and causal). I sometimes expand those realms to five (matter, body, mind, soul, and spirit), but I am willing to strongly defend only the former. That is, I claim that every major human culture, at least by the time of *Homo sapiens*, recognized these three main realms of existence (as evidenced also in waking, dreaming, and sleeping). That is almost the only item of the "perennial philosophy" that I have defended. Most of the other aspects of the traditional version of the perennial philosophy (as maintained by, e.g., Frithjof Schuon, Ananda Coomaraswamy, Henry Corbin, Seyyed Nasr, Huston Smith, Marco Pallis, René Guénon, etc.)—aspects such as unchanging archetypes, involution and evolution as fixed and predetermined, the strictly hierarchical (as opposed to holonic/quadratic) nature of reality, etc.—I do not believe are either universal or true, and I have sharply distanced myself from those theorists in that regard.

Although I have been a harsh critic of the perennial philosophy, I still believe that, especially in its most sophisticated forms, it is a fountain of unsurpassed wisdom, even if we have to dust it off a bit. For a genuine T.O.E., I believe we need a judicious blend of the best of premodern, modern, and postmodern, which is the explicit task of SES and all post-SES books.

17. Narrow religion, in one sense, is simply the worldview of any stage of development. There is purple religion, red religion, blue religion, orange religion, green religion, and so on. Narrow religion attempts to offer meaning and solace to the self at any given level. (Deep religion, on the other hand, attempts to change levels altogether, moving the self—either temporarily or permanently—into psychic, subtle, causal, or nondual realms. Again, this is the difference between legitimate and authentic religion, as described in *A Sociable God* [CW3]).

Narrow religion is what we mean when we say that somebody has "got" religion or believes in something "religiously"—the belief does not actually have to be religious in content, but simply be embraced intensely. *Star Trek* fans say that logic is Spock's religion, for example. When the self identifies with a particular level or wave of development, the self religiously believes in the worldview of that level and holds onto it for dear life. This intense identification, at any level, generates the narrow "religion" of that level, or the emotional attachment and identification with the worldview of that level, which the self necessarily feels at each of its waves of unfoldings (until it can disidentify with that level and move on to the next, which it then religiously embraces. This process continues until developmental arrest sets in, or one develops into the soul and spirit realms, there to discover deep spirituality and the divine self: one's narrow religion has become deep religion).

A few quick examples of the narrow religion of each wave of existence: Purple religion includes some forms of voodoo and the belief in word magic. Red religion is a religion of archetypal mythic beliefs with an emphasis on the magical power of the archetypal figures (Moses parted the Red Sea, Christ was born from a virgin, Lao Tzu was 900 years old when he was born, etc.). Blue religion is a religion of law and order, a mythic-membership structure that binds people together through obedience to a great Order or Other; it is authoritarian, rigidly hierarchical, and uses guilt as social control (the Ten Commandments, the Analects of Confucius, much of the Koran, etc.); but it does extend care to all those who embrace the mythic beliefs (while all those who do not are eternally damned). Orange religion is a religion of positivism and scientific materialism; its advocates believe this worldview just as religiously as do any fundamentalists, and they have their own skeptical Inquisitors who will attack and ridicule the worldviews of any of the other levels. (Auguste Comte, the father of modern scientific positivism, actually proposed having—and these are his words—a "Pope of Positivism," which is a fine example of the narrow religion possible at the egoic-rational level. This, again, would be Spock's "religion.") But orange religion is also the beginning of the belief in equal rights for all individuals, regardless of race, color, creed, or gender. Green religion extends that to a kindness and subjective caring for all souls and a sensitivity to all of the earth's inhabitants (although it turns very mean—the "mean green meme"— toward all those who do not share its religion of politically correct views). Second-tier religion is a religion of holism, cosmic oneness, and universal pattern (as Beck and Cowan put it, second tier believes that "the earth is one organism with a collective mind"). Moving beyond even that integral *belief* in cosmic oneness, psychic religion is an *actual experience* of this cosmic oneness (a type of nature mysticism). Subtle religion is a direct experience of the divine Ground of this cosmic order (deity mysticism). And causal religion is a direct experience of the radically infinite and unqualifiable nature of this Ground (formless mysticism).

Narrow religion, then, is simply those beliefs, practices, customs, experiences, and traditions that help one to translate and embrace the worldview of any given wave; whereas deep religion involves those practices, techniques, and traditions that help one to transform to the higher, transrational, transpersonal waves (psychic, subtle, causal, and nondual; by any other names, soul and spirit). And these deep-spirituality practices disclose actual realities; they are tapping into genuine truths. These deep-spirituality practices are therefore also known (in part) as contemplative sciences—or simply good science—because they are not merely beliefs but actual practices, grounded in injunctions, experiential evidence, and peer review. They are repeatable, shareable, public practices that disclose realities, that is, actual truths, and not merely cultural meanings, local value structures, and so on. These higher waves are as true as are the blue, orange, or green waves. If you believe that there is decent evidence for those waves, the same applies to these transpersonal waves that claim to experience the Divine directly.

18. Does this mean that stages are being skipped? Not at all, because to say that the pre-Enlightenment world was, for example, at the blue wave, only means that the *average* level of consciousness was blue. Individuals could be at much higher or much lower waves in their own case, and, building upon second tier or universal consciousness, many mystics evolved into psychic, subtle, and causal waves. But society at large did not support the higher waves, and hence their achievement was difficult outside of protected enclaves or communities and was thus much rarer, being confined mostly to great shamans, saints, and sages. See *Integral Psychology* for a full discussion of this theme, as well as a summary of the massive amounts of cross-cultural evidence for these higher waves of development.

19. In the terms of note 17, we can say: with the Enlightenment, the orange narrow religion of scientific materialism took up a brutally adversarial stance toward the blue narrow religion of the church.

20. For a discussion of postliberal spirituality, see *The Eye of Spirit* (CW7), *The Marriage of Sense and Soul* (CW8), and *Boomeritis*.

Chapter 5: The Real World

1. Flatland is explained in *The Marriage of Sense and Soul*, and in more detail in SES and *Brief History*. I use the term in two senses: (1) Technically, it is the belief that only Right-Hand realities are irreducibly real; it is the reduction of all Left-Hand events to their Right-Hand correlates. (2) I also use the word "flatland" to mean any Left-Hand belief that either comes from, or believes only in, one particular level of consciousness. Thus, behaviorists are flatland in the first sense (they believe only in objectively observable behavior), and pluralistic relativists are flatland in the second (they acknowledge only the values of the green meme).

    Within flatland reductionism (in the first sense), there are two degrees: subtle reductionism, which reduces everything to the Lower-Right quadrant (e.g., dynamical process systems, chaos and complexity theories, traditional systems theory, social autopoiesis, the Web of Life, etc.), and gross reductionism, which goes even further and reduces those objective systems to objective atoms (reduces all phenomena to atomistic units in the Upper Right). Subtle reductionism is also known as exterior holism or flatland holism (in contrast to integral holism, which unites both interior holism and exterior holism). Both gross and subtle reductionism believe the entire world can be accounted for in third-person it-language (i.e., they are both monological, not dialogical or translogical). The "crime of the Enlightenment," incidentally, was subtle reductionism, not gross reductionism. The Enlightenment philosophers were often great systems thinkers; they were the first great proponents of the *System de la Nature* and the "great interlocking order" (Charles Taylor, *Sources of the Self*; see also SES, chaps. 12 and 13).

2. This "blank slate" view of the human mind—with its correlates in a psychology of behaviorism and associationism, and an epistemology of empiricism—was adopted by liberalism for many reasons, not the least of which was that it promised the "unlimited perfectibility" of human beings through various types of objective social engineering. All innate differences, capacities, and structures were summarily rejected, and human beings, born in a state rather akin to a blob of clay, could thus be molded by exterior institutions and forces (behaviorism, associationism) into any desired state.

David Hartley, in his *Observations on Man* (1749), had worked out a psychological theory (associationism) that viewed the mind as assembly of sensations; this fit well the empirical theories of epistemology (Locke, Berkeley, Hume); and the entire general package was made to order for the rising political theories of liberalism. James Mill and his son John Stuart Mill embraced these ideas for a simple reason: "In psychology," John wrote of his father, "his fundamental doctrine was the formation of all human character by circumstances [objective causation], through the universal principle of association, and the consequent unlimited possibility of improving the moral and intellectual condition of mankind. . . ." This improvement could occur by behavioristic education, where the proper exteriors are imprinted on the interiors; or, especially in later versions, by more aggressive social engineering (which is why behaviorism—no matter how crude and incorrect in most respects—remained the state psychology of the Soviet Union, and it remains the implicit psychology of many forms of traditional liberalism).

As John Passmore (*A Hundred Years of Philosophy*) points out: "In one of his earliest speeches, [John Stuart] Mill announced that he shared his father's belief in perfectibility; that same faith is no less strongly expressed in the last of Mill's writings. Innate differences he always rejected out of hand, never more passionately than in his *The Subjection of Women* (1869), in which he argued that even 'the least contestable differences' between the sexes are such that they may 'very well have been produced by circumstances [objective causation] without any differences of natural capacity [subjective causation].'" Always there is the blank slate, into which a more perfect world will be poured from the outside, with no thought that there might be realities on the interior that need to be addressed as well. The "blank slate" meant radical social policy. "Associationism, in Mill's eyes, is not merely a psychological hypothesis, to be candidly examined as such: it is the essential presumption of a radical social policy."

The same was true for empiricism: not just an epistemology, but a blueprint for social action, based almost entirely on objective causation (and an implicit denial of subjective causation), which was one of the main motives for adopting it. "Empiricism, similarly, is more than an epistemological analysis; not to be an empiricist is to adhere to 'the Establishment'—to be committed to the 'sacred' doctrines and institutions." To believe in anything other than empiricism is, says Mill, "the great intellectual support of false doctrines and bad institutions." Empiricism is thus the doorway to molding human beings in an unlimited fashion (hence "perfectibility" as a social engineering agenda).

On the one hand, as we will see, this was a noble effort to move from ethnocentric notions of innate but often discriminatory "differences" (e.g., heathens are born without a soul) to a worldcentric, postconventional morality as free of prejudice and bias as possible (this is a motive I share). The fact is, much of "the Establishment"—which in Mill's time meant the mythic-membership, ethnocentric doctrines of the Church (the "sacred institutions")—are in fact in need of critical review, and empiricism can most definitely assist us in doing so (it challenges the empirical claims of narrow religion). On the other hand, however, by denying that the interiors themselves have realities, realms, stages, and states of their own—and by, in fact, reducing them to imprints of the sensorimotor world—liberal philosophy and psychology would deeply sabotage their own goals. They would, with their allegiance to merely sensory empiricism and the blank slate, be prime contributors to the worldview of scientific materialism, a flatland view of the universe that in fact acts to undermine and sometimes grossly derail genuine growth and development of the interior domains. If there is an "unlimited perfectibility" of human beings, it lies not just in developing exteriors, but also in understanding the spiral of interior development. As we will see throughout this chapter, the liberal "blank slate" nobly aimed for worldcentric moral consciousness—and then crippled the path to it.

3. This is why the more "liberal" or "permissive" a society becomes, the less liberalism can flourish. When all stances are taken to be equal, and "no judgments" are made toward various stances—none are to be "marginalized"—then egocentric and ethnocentric are allowed to flourish, at which point the very existence of worldcentric liberalism becomes deeply threatened. Traditional liberalism works to undermine the foundations of traditional liberalism. See *One Taste*, October 3 and 15, December 10; and *Boomeritis*.

4. Because the mythic-membership wave (the blue meme) is a normal and nec-

essary wave of human development, a truly integral politics, based on the prime directive, would realize the absolutely necessary (if limited) role of the blue meme in any society, and not simply try to dissolve it, which the liberal green meme does every chance it gets. Green dissolves blue, which is one of the true political nightmares in this country and abroad.

5. Thus, Integral Politics attempts to integrate political orientations across the spectrum of at least three major areas of an all-quadrant, all-level model: social causation, individual/collective, and levels of development. There are a few other areas that need not be addressed in this simple introduction, such as the direction of change (regressive, progressive, stationary; e.g., recaptured goodness vs. growth to goodness), methods of change (critical, translative, transformative), and types of freedom (negative, positive). The following three areas are the most significant:

(1) *Social causation.* If a person is suffering, disadvantaged, or disenfranchised, where should we look for the basic cause: in the person himself, or in the social organization? Nature or nurture? Internal causation or external causation? Liberals tend to look for the cause of suffering in objective social institutions: people suffer because society is unjust. You are poor because you have been oppressed, marginalized, or disenfranchised; or, at the least, you are poor because you have not been given a fair chance (e.g., J. S. Mill). Conservatives, on the other hand, tend to situate the main cause in the person himself: you are poor because you are lazy. Conservatives blame interior factors for much of human suffering; social institutions do not repress people as much as help them rise to their greater potentials (e.g., Edmund Burke). For conservatives, the basic cause of suffering is thus something in the individual, not in his or her surroundings, upbringing, or social institutions.

This definition of liberal and conservative was first explicitly set forth in *Up from Eden* (1981) and has since become quite popular. Here is an example from Lance Morrow, reviewing David Horowitz's book *Hating Whitey* in *Time* magazine (November 22, 1999). "This is the line between what might be called the Externalists and the Internalists. Externalists, who tend toward the political left, say that America's racial problems are to be addressed through outside interventions (affirmative action, busing and other government programs to repair the damage of the past and enforce racial justice). Internalists, who are apt to be conservative, stress solutions that require efforts from the inside: education, hard work, self-motivation, morale, bourgeois values, deferred gratification, the old immigrant virtues." This distinction—internal versus external causation—is one dimension of an integral politics.

(2) *Individual/collective.* In arranging the just society, should more emphasis be placed on the individual or on the collective? This is a centuries-old dilemma, but came into prominence with the rise of the Enlightenment and the individualized self, a rather recent emergence (see *Up from Eden*). Lawrence Chickering, in *Beyond Left and Right*, calls these the "freedom"

and "order" wings of any political party. Couple this with the definitions of liberal (Left) and conservative (Right) given above, and we have a specific version of free and order Left, and free and order Right orientations. (See note 8 for the Chickering/Sprecher matrix.)

Thus, for example, economic libertarians tend to be free Right (free, because they place more emphasis on individual freedoms; Right, because they believe in internal causation: you are poor because you aren't working hard enough. Therefore, government should keep its hands off the marketplace and let the market reward individual initiative). Traditional conservatives are order Right (order, because they place emphasis on collective values, civic virtue, family values, etc.; and Right because they believe in internal causation: what's wrong with this society is that individuals don't have enough traditional values instilled in them, so start school prayer, champion the work ethic, support family values, etc.).

The classic liberal of the Enlightenment was free Left (free, in that individual freedoms were championed in the face of the herd mentality and ethnocentric religion; Left, in that the cause of human suffering is corrupt and repressive social institutions; all humans are born equal, but society treats them unfairly. This free-Left orientation was thus often a revolutionary politics—if society is unjust, get rid of it, which France and America did). Civil libertarians carry on this free-Left orientation, arguing the free rights of individuals over almost any challenge.

Green liberals are almost always order Left: they want their values—whether multicultural, feminist, or otherwise—imposed on society as a whole, through both education and governmental action. This is why order Right and order Left have often joined forces to make the strangest bedfellows. For example, some conservatives and some radical feminists have both called for bans on pornography: what they have in common is their willingness to impose their values on others, which overrides their liberal and conservative differences.

It has been generally noted that liberalism started out free Left—arguing that government should stay out of the lives of individuals—and slowly tended to become order Left—arguing that big government must interfere with individuals on a daily basis, for moral reasons. The standard example is civil rights: if government had not intervened, we would still have segregation. There is clearly some truth to this. However, just as clearly, order Left—in addition to its healthy and important contributions—is also the major home of boomeritis (postconventional green pluralism infected with preconventional narcissism), and boomeritis wants to interfere with peoples' lives just for the power of it all. Order Left has thus become the home of boomeritis feminism, boomeritis multiculturalism, boomeritis ecology (aka ecofascism), and so on. For integrating free and order (or agency and communion), see note 7.

(3) *Levels of development.* The last major area is the general wave of existence that a political orientation tends to address. Thus, conservatives

tend to champion the conventional waves (blue to orange), and liberals tend to champion the nonconventional waves (purple/red and orange/green).

Integral Politics makes two basic claims. One, using those three major dimensions (and other minor ones briefly noted at the beginning), the full spectrum of political orientations can be mapped. Two, there is a way to fully integrate all of those political orientations (not in their extremist versions, but in their healthy versions). For these three major dimensions, this means, respectively: (1) placing an emphasis on both interior and exterior causation, thus supporting both interior and exterior development; (2) recognizing a participatory democracy where the individual can feel that he or she is the author of the collective laws regulating his or her behavior; (3) recognizing the prime directive across the entire spiral of development.

In order to integrate all three of these dimensions in a coherent fashion, we need an underlying philosophy that can display the exact relation of these dimensions to each other in an integral way. I have attempted to present such an integral philosophy—called "all-quadrant, all-level"—in a series of books, of which this book is a simple introduction. (For further reflections on Integral Politics, see *Boomeritis*.) Using this model, these dimensions can be fully integrated theoretically; it now remains to translate this into a political *practice* uniting the best of conservatism and liberalism—an integration that will ride the wave of the integral future.

6. The prime directive also decisively sides with a growth-to-goodness model, not a recaptured-goodness model (See *One Taste*, December 10 entry, and *Boomeritis*). The traditional liberal believes in a state of "original goodness," which corrupt social institutions repress and oppress. While there is some truth to that notion (as explained in the *One Taste* entry), psychological research has decisively sided with the growth-to-goodness model, which points out that development generally unfolds from preconventional to conventional to postconventional. Along with "blank slate" humans, mere empiricist epistemology, and behavioristic psychology, the liberal version of "original goodness" has not found support in extensive research, leaving traditional liberalism without a believable philosophy, psychology, or ethics. An all-quadrant, all-level approach attempts to ground the noble aims of liberalism in a sturdier foundation, combined with the best of the conservative tradition.

As for "stages of the interior," this actually means *stages in all of the quadrants*—subjective (intentional), objective (behavioral), intersubjective (cultural), and interobjective (social). The waves of development unfold in all four quadrants, and all four of those dimensions need to be taken into account. Moreover, there can be uneven development between the quadrants—highly developed technology (its) can be given to poorly developed, ethnocentric cultures (we), with nightmarish results (e.g., Kosovo)—and so on.

Thus, I technically give the two steps toward an Integral Politics as: (I) uniting interior and exterior; (II) understanding stages of both and thus arriving at the prime directive. Of course, *all* dimensions outlined in note 5 are essential for a truly Integrated Politics, but these are two of the most pressing.

These two steps, in practice, have slightly different manifestations for liberals and conservatives, since both of those political philosophies need to follow the two steps by supplementing their agenda with that which they presently lack. *For most conservatives* (who believe in interior causation and in stages of the interior, but only up to mythic-membership or blue/orange), Stage I means being more willing to recognize the partial but genuine importance of exterior causation in many circumstances and thus to act "more compassionately" toward the disadvantaged (hence, "compassionate conservatism"). Stage II—which has not yet been taken—involves moving from mythic-membership values to worldcentric values, not by abandoning the former but by enriching them (by supplements from the higher, post-blue stages).

For most liberals (who believe in exterior causation and in no stages of the interior), Stage I means acknowledging interior causation in the first place. Bill Clinton's synthesis of "opportunity and responsibility" (as applied to welfare reform and other issues) did just that; this was an innovative departure from traditional liberalism, because the "responsibility" part acknowledged interior causation (people, not institutions, are partly responsible for their own disadvantage). The joining of "responsibility" (provided by the person) and "opportunity" (provided by the government) was thus an attempt to unite interior and exterior, and this is Clinton's version of Stage I (as pointed out to me by Drexel Sprecher). Stage II—which has not yet been taken—involves recognizing not just the interior, but stages of the interior (the irony, again, is that the traditional liberal stance itself already comes from the worldcentric stage, so this is not as daunting a challenge as it might seem; all that is required, in this case, is that liberals acknowledge a more accurate self-conception of their own stance and the developmental stages that produced it).

At this moment in 2000, both parties have attempted some form of Stage I; neither party has attempted Stage II, although both are struggling toward it. Right now it is a horse race to see whether liberalism or conservatism can more readily recognize and address their traditional deficiencies and thus arrive at a more genuinely integral politics. Will it be harder for traditional conservatives to move from mythic-membership to worldcentric, or harder for liberals to acknowledge stages of the interior? The party that can better address its deficiencies will arrive at a political conception of the second stage of an integral politics, will therefore more fully understand and implement the prime directive (which embraces the greatest depth for the greatest span), and will thus have the inside track in the political arena for the foreseeable future.

7. On the integration of free (autonomous) and order (communion): "Autonomy" is an unfortunate word in almost every way. One, there is no

fully autonomous finite self, only a relatively autonomous self (although the relative autonomy increases at every wave). Two, the relatively autonomous self of every stage is set in vast networks of relationships and processes (natural, objective, cultural, social)—in short, agency is always agency-in-communion—which makes mockery of "autonomy" or isolated agency in general. Three, the relatively autonomous self of every stage also exists in a *system of exchanges* with other relatively autonomous selves at a *similar level* of development.

The latter point is particularly important. The purple self exists in a system of mutual exchanges with other purple selves, the blue self exists in a system of mutual exchanges with other blue selves, the orange self with other orange selves, the green self with other green selves, and so on. (Of course, blue also interacts with purple, red, orange, green, yellow, etc. It is just that each level of self particularly recognizes itself in exchanges with other selves of similar depth.) In short, the self at every level is a self-in-relationship-with-other-selves (agency-in-communion).

This gives us purchase on the raging debate between liberals and communitarians: both of them have an important but partial piece of the puzzle. The communitarians are right that the self is always a situated or saturated self—it is always a self-in-context (or agency-in-communion, or autonomy-in-relationship). But the liberals are right in that the orange self has relatively *more autonomy* than the blue self, and that greater relative autonomy must be protected from the herd mentality of blue (hence liberal rights). But the relatively autonomous liberal (orange) self is still a self-in-relationship and it recognizes itself only in exchanges with other relatively autonomous selves. Thus, the autonomy of one level is relatively greater than that of a previous level, but autonomy is always autonomy-in-relationship (agency is always agency-in-communion). Even the highly integral or "autonomous self" (in fig. 2-1) seeks out relationships with other autonomous selves. That is, agency seeks agency of similar depth and depends upon that relationship for mutual recognition, which is a genuine need of the self at every level. In the early stages of development, those relationships are mandatory for self formation; in the adult, those relationships are necessary for the self's happiness and wellbeing, and for its actual existence in mutual recognition. Of course the adult self can live without those relationships—if it is stranded on a desert island, for example—but the self simply withers in such aridity.

The typical liberal notion of autonomy *correctly* understood the relative increase in autonomy of the orange self over the blue self—and *correctly* demanded a system of rights to protect orange individuality from blue oppression—but then *incorrectly* assumed that such autonomy was an atomistic freedom. Liberal theory misunderstood autonomy as atomism (or isolated agency) and thus it fundamentally misunderstood the nature of the self—which is always agency-in-communion—and thus it likewise misunderstood the nature of society, which is not a contract between atomistic selves but an inescapable manifestation of agency-in-communion.

As described in both *Sex, Ecology, Spirituality* and *Brief History*, agency means *rights*, and communion means *responsibilities*, and thus agency-in-communion means that each self (at whatever level) is always a series of rights-in-responsibilities or freedom-with-duties. But the Enlightenment liberal self (orange) identified itself *only* with rights and freedoms, and identified blue only with duties and responsibilities, and thus in its noble attempt to protect the orange self from the blue herd—which really meant, protect orange agency-in-communion from blue agency-in-communion (or protect orange rights-in-responsibilities from blue rights-in-responsibilities)—the orange self severed rights from responsibilities, identified itself with rights and blue with responsibilities, and thus in protecting orange from blue inadvertently imagined it could have rights without responsibilities, agency without communion, freedom without obligations, whoopee without duty. And in that regard, liberal notions of autonomy indeed contributed to regressive, narcissistic, egocentric disintegration of social communion, caring, and obligation.

Thus, one of the first items on the agenda of a truly integral politics is to reconnect rights and responsibilities at a postconventional level (orange and higher), without regressing to merely blue rights-and-responsibilities. For the liberal autonomous self exists only in a network of mutual exchanges with other autonomous selves, and that network of agency-in-communion imposes new duties and responsibilities even as it opens new freedoms and opportunities: both must be fully honored. (See *Up from Eden* for a discussion of relational exchange at each level of selfhood; see *Sex, Ecology, Spirituality* and *A Brief History of Everything* for a discussion of agency-in-communion as rights-in-responsibilities.)

8. Although neither Sprecher nor Chickering has at this time formally published this definition of Left and Right, Sprecher asserts that he independently arrived at it a year or so after I did, which I accept. Combining this definition of liberal and conservative with order and freedom gives a matrix of order and free Left, order and free Right, which is often known as the Chickering/Sprecher matrix (see note 5).

Sprecher is the originator of two specialized integral disciplines: generative leadership (emphasizing subjective development) and decentralized and integrated governance (emphasizing objective development). He has also designed an influential approach to political leadership training that includes exercises with injunctions, experiences, and verification to teach integral insights.

Although the two steps toward a more integral politics, as they are stated in note 6, are my own ("uniting interior and exterior; seeing stages of both and thus arriving at the prime directive"), Sprecher has independently arrived at a somewhat similar conception (and considerably spurred my own articulation), although Sprecher specifically refers to his approach as "Third Way." He sees the "two steps" toward the Third Way as being primarily economic and horizontal, then cultural and vertical. The first is the horizontal integration of the Left and Right, the second is the vertical integration of order and freedom. Many of these important issues will be dealt with in a forthcoming American Renaissance paper called "The Future of the Third Way," authored by Sprecher with input from Chickering and myself.

9. Thus, if individuals are *order Left*, e.g., socialist (order = puts importance on the lower or collective quadrants, and Left = puts importance in exterior causation or Right-Hand quadrants), then they put most of their emphasis on factors in the Lower Right (the economic and objective social system), and they wish government intervention in that quadrant (e.g., welfare statism). If individuals are *order Right*, e.g., traditionalist or fundamentalist (order = lower or collective, and Right = a belief in interior causation or Left-Hand quadrants), then they put most of their emphasis on the Lower Left (cultural beliefs and worldviews) and insist that everybody comply with their norms and values, by government intervention if necessary (e.g., school prayer). If individuals are *free Right*, e.g., economic libertarian (free = upper or individual, and Right = a belief in interior causation or Left-Hand realities), they put most of their emphasis on the Upper-Left quadrant: individuals must assume responsibility for their own success, and government should therefore stay out of interfering with the Right-Hand (e.g., economic) quadrants altogether (except to protect those rights and freedoms). If individuals are *free Left*, e.g., civil libertarian, they put most of their emphasis on the freedom of individual behavior (Upper Right), and government should intervene only to protect those freedoms. There are many variations on those themes, and we must also take the developmental levels themselves into account, but those simple examples indicate the importance of a more integral analysis.

10. An integral approach to world governance would stem in part from what Clare Graves called the "second tier" of psychological development, yellow and turquoise. (Many different theorists speak of several tiers—first, second, third, fourth, and so on. The simple Gravesian two-tier conception works just fine for the point I am making; in the next chapter we will add "third tier" for transpersonal realities, which begin with coral/psychic.) Using the terms of Spiral Dynamics, the United States Constitution was the culmination and brilliant high point of first-tier governance (stemming generally from orange-to-green principles), and it established the governance systems for corporate states (and to some degree value communities). Now, in the postnational and postgreen world, we need a governance system for a world Civilization (see chap. 6), which will allow global and holistic meshworks to flourish. I believe, of course, that it will be an "all-quadrant, all-level" approach, guided by the Basic Moral Intuition ("protect and promote the greatest depth for the greatest span"), which itself embodies both the prime directive (facilitate the health of the entire spiral of development without unduly privileging any particular wave) and a gentle pacer of transformation for the full spectrum of human resources (inviting people to grow and devel-

op their full potentials—interior and exterior—to the best of their abilities). Those items—the integral approach, the BMI, the prime directive, and a pacer of transformation—are key ingredients, I believe, in any second-tier or integral self-governance. The translation of these ideas into a set of world governance meshworks—which would fully accept the differentiation of national governments but also allow their integration and mutual facilitation—remains the great challenge of millennial politics.

11. See the works of Larry Dossey, Jon Kabat-Zinn, Jeanne Achterberg, Ken Pelletier, Joan Borysenko, among others.

12. John Astin, "The Integral Philosophy of Ken Wilber: Contributions to the Study of CAM [Complementary and Alternative Medicine] and Conventional Medicine," in preparation.

13. "Sensorimotor Sequencing," presented at the Psychological Trauma conference, sponsored by Boston University School of Medicine and Harvard Medical School.

14. G. Schwartz and L. Russek, "The Challenge of One Medicine: Theories of Health and Eight World Hypotheses," *Advances: The Journal of Mind-Body Health*.

15. See L. Dossey, "The Great Chain of Healing: Toward an Integral Vision of Medicine (With a Bow to Ken Wilber)," in Crittenden et al. (eds.), *Kindred Visions*, forthcoming from Shambhala.

16. D. Paulson, "Management: A Multidimensional/Multilevel Perspective," in Crittenden et al. (eds.), *Kindred Visions*, forthcoming from Shambhala. See also D. Paulson, *Topical Antimicrobial Testing and Evaluation*, Marcel Dekker, 1999; "Successfully Marketing Skin Moisturizing Products," *Soap/Cosmetics/Chemical Specialties*, August 1999; "Developing Effective Topical Antimicrobials," *Soap/Cosmetics/Chemical Specialties*, December 1997. Daryl has published extensively on "all-quadrant, all-level" applications in various fields, including a widely appreciated elucidation of near-death experiences ("The Near-Death Experience: An Integration of Cultural, Spiritual, and Physical Perspectives," *Journal of Near Death Studies*, 18 (1), Fall 1999). Daryl is also on the FDA's panel of experts on food safety. "We use the quadrant model to reduce infections such as *Escherichia coli* outbreaks of strain 0157-H7."

When it comes to the "all-level" part in human beings, you can use any of the reputable developmental models, from Maslow to Graves to Loevinger. Spiral Dynamics has had a great deal of success in this regard, and it now uses an "all-quadrant, all-level" refinement of its own system (quite similar to that depicted in fig. 3-1).

17. G. Gioja, "Creating Leaders (Beyond Transformation: An Integral Manifesto)"; On Purpose Associates (Cleveland et al.), "The Practical Philosopher: How Ken Wilber Changed Our Practice"; and L. Burke, "Not Just Money, Meaning," are all in Crittenden et al. (eds.), *Kindred Visions*, forthcoming from Shambhala. The quote from The Leadership Circle (Bob Anderson, Jim Stuart, and Eric Klein) is taken from "The Leadership Circle:

Bringing Spiritual Intelligence to the Work"; they can be contacted through Klein's publisher (*Awakening Corporate Soul*).

18. Of the many ecotheorists who have begun using a more integral approach, special mention might be made of the work of Matthew Kalman, Michael Zimmerman (*Radical Ecology*), and Gus diZerega. DiZerega and I have had our theoretical differences, but I believe we now see eye to eye on many ecological issues, and in fact we have planned some joint publications. The core of Gus's previous complaint about my work was that, because I suggested that many individuals involved in nature mysticism are often involved in prerational and even regressive occasions, I was saying that all nature mysticism is such, which is definitely not my opinion, as Gus now acknowledges. I do not mean to imply that Gus would agree with all my points, but I believe it is safe to say that he is comfortable with an all-quadrant, all-level approach that includes nature mysticism, deity mysticism, formless mysticism, and nondual mysticism (psychic, subtle, causal, nondual). We also both share an appreciation of the some of the many positive gains of modernity and the Enlightenment, in addition to understanding their downsides, on which most ecotheories unfairly focus.

19. This sounds a little bit like liberal inclusiveness, except that the traditional liberal, who ignores or denies stages of interior development, cannot easily accept many of the natural and necessary stages of interior development (particularly the conformist, law-and-order, fundamentalist stage) through which all normal human beings progress, and thus liberals act to dissolve these crucially important structures wherever they find them, which has a profoundly disruptive and regressive effect. As Spiral Dynamics puts it, green dissolves blue, and thus green often has an incredibly harmful effect on the prime directive, not only at home but in foreign policy (e.g., trying to push green "human rights" on countries that are at blue is, at best a waste of time, and at paradoxical worst, a reactionary endeavor. You handle blue rigidity not with green sensitivity but with, e.g., orange technology).
    Theorists sympathetic to a more integral orientation toward minorities (and developing countries) include Beck, Connie Hilliard, and Maureen Silos. Contributions by all of them can be found in *Kindred Visions*, Crittenden et al. (eds.), forthcoming from Shambhala.

20. Note the emphasis on the two stages of a more integral politics: acknowledging the interior, then acknowledging waves of the interior.

21. The problem with Artificial Intelligence (AI) and robotics is that most of its advocates are naive psychologists with an astonishingly impoverished view of consciousness, what it is and how it develops. If you look at the UL quadrant in figure 4-4, you can trace the history (and the constitutive holons) of human consciousness: the prehension of atoms and molecules is taken up and into the irritability of cells, which is taken up and into the sensations of neuronal organisms, which are taken up and into the perceptions of animals with neural cords, which are taken up and into the impulses of animals with reptilian brain stems, which are taken up and into the emotions and feelings

of animals with limbic systems, which are taken up and into the symbols and concepts of animals with a neocortex, at which point the complex neocortex, in certain human brains, can produce formal operational thinking or logic. But each and every one of those holons, enfolded into its successors, is a crucial part of the net result, human consciousness.

Yet computer programmers tend to focus on the type of consciousness that they know best—namely, logical and mathematical—and they "skim off" this thin, outer film of consciousness and program some of its rules and algorithms into a computer, and they imagine that this superficial, disembodied, abstract, dissociated, artificial intelligence is actually the same thing as human consciousness. And they naturally think that, given another decade or two, "human consciousness" will be able to be downloaded into silicon chips and thus achieve an eternal life, whereas all that is being downloaded is their own thin, abstract, dissociated consciousness.

In order to produce an artificial intelligence that is truly human-like, AI engineers would have to be able to recreate the consciousness of each and every holon making up the superholon of human consciousness. They would have to be able to create and animate everything from cell irritability to reptilian instincts to limbic-system emotions to neocortex rationality and connectivity (a neocortex that has more neuronal connections than there are stars in the known universe). AI is not even close to being able to recreate organic cell irritability, so we can, for the foreseeable future, ignore its other grandiose claims. Robotics through the next century will be confined to behaviors that can be programmed according to certain specific algorithms, logical-digital rules, some types of fuzzy logic, and neural learning networks that still replicate only the most surface forms of consciousness.

There is another major difficulty: consciousness is a four-quadrant affair. AI is trying to program merely UR-quadrant behavioral rules and learning mechanisms, and that will never produce the four-quadrant thing we call real consciousness. A subset of this argument is John Searle's, which in effect says that UR behavior will never be the same thing as UL intentionality. He is quite right; and UR behavior will never produce intersubjective cultural values, either (LL).

Finally, there is the argument from deep-spirituality itself: consciousness is not the product of anything, whether *that* be human brains or robots. Pure consciousness is instead the Source and Ground of all manifestation, and if you think you can put *that* into a computer. . . . The computer is a manifestation of consciousness, not vice versa, and all that you can get into (or out of) a computer is, again, nothing but a thin, partial, superficial slice of the incredible Kosmic Pie. Besides, this whole notion that consciousness can be downloaded into microchips comes mostly from geeky adolescent males who can't get laid and stay up all hours of the night staring into a computer screen, dissociating, abstracting, dissolved in disembodied thinking. I'm a geek myself, so don't get me wrong, but please. . . . There are more holons in human consciousness than are dreamt of in AI.

22. Edwin Firmage, *Leaving the Fold*, J. Ure (ed.), p. 229.

23. In the main text I suggested that a combination of both exterior/legal constraints and interior/moral wisdom—or, more generally, an integral approach—will be necessary to face these challenges. This is basically the same as saying that second-tier governance systems will necessarily be involved (since only at second tier do truly integral solutions become available). The likely fact is that, for the foreseeable future, the bulk of humanity will be at pre-worldcentric waves (egocentric and ethnocentric), and thus a second-tier world governance meshwork will have to be implemented in order to meet these challenges. This is analogous to the U.S. Constitution, which, as we noted, was a moral-stage-5 document that governed a people where less than 10 percent of its population was actually at stage 5. Just so, a second-tier world governance meshwork will have to facilitate integration of a world where less than 10 percent of its population is actually at second tier. Exactly how this will happen, we cannot say at this moment, because an integral politics is just beginning to emerge, and all complex emergences are inherently unpredictable in final form. That it will happen is virtually certain (if we survive that long); how and when and where: these will surprise us to some degree (if we are not surprised, it is not a true emergent). Still, many of its general features can be outlined, and many of the facilitating factors that will make its emergence more likely can now be identified. The Institute of Integral Politics has this as one of its foremost policy issues.

   Joe Firmage (cofounder of USWeb/CKS, Intend Change, and Project Voyager, and a strong supporter and member of Integral Institute), points out that there are two general sides to this governance issue—which he calls "coercive" and "noncoercive"—again, external legal control backed by force and internal moral wisdom providing self-guidance—and the question is, what is the right and proper balance of these two forms of constraint for the coming nightmares that a lack of integral development has caused? On the one hand are forms of "decentralized and integrated" governance systems, being explored by several members of Integral Institute; in Firmage's version: "New feasibilities in ideotechnomics can enable new holistic individual priorities, which can enable the evolution of governance into a smaller, less controlling, but more consistent and service-oriented role." And on the other hand, we must also look to a renewed attention to interior development, including full-spectrum education, engaged public awareness, integral political leadership, and deep spirituality. In Firmage's view, "From my vantage point, nothing less than an integral spiritual revolution will suffice, since no form of exterior control mechanism could completely work, and any that would come close would make life unlivable."

   This balanced integration of exterior development with interior development is, of course, simply another version of integral politics, and it now seems certain that only with integral political approaches can these problems even be framed in an intelligent fashion. (See notes 5, 6, 7, 8, and 10.) But one inviolate conclusion now stands forth: The coercive aspects required by world governance will rise in direct proportion to the lack of interior development.

CHAPTER 6: MAPS OF THE KOSMOS

1. One reviewer chastised me for using "holistic" instead of my own "holonic." The reviewer agreed with me that there are several major flaws in most forms of holism—which stresses "the Whole"—and these inadequacies are overcome with a holonic approach—which stresses both wholes and parts, or whole/parts, or holons. This is true. Still, although there are important differences between holistic and holonic models, I often use both words synonymously, because "holonic" is not a well-known term.

2. See SES, *Brief History*, and *The Marriage of Sense and Soul* for an account of the strengths and weaknesses of Idealism.

3. Schwartz et al. suggest that a holonic model can embrace all eight. See G. Schwartz, C. Santerre, and L. Russek, "Bringing Order to the Whole: Eight World Hypotheses Applied to Ken Wilber's Integral Approach to Consciousness," in Crittenden et al., *Kindred Visions*, forthcoming from Shambhala.

4. This is obviously a useful scheme, and it can be made even more germane by what I call a cross-level analysis. This is a very important addition that is discussed in detail in note 19.

5. See *One Taste*, October 3 and 15 entries, for a further discussion of why the notion of development is crucial to being able to integrate various worldviews. For the chakra levels, see note 18.

   Of course, if junior-level worldviews make claims about senior levels, they have to be tested using the criteria of the senior levels. For example, if astrology makes rational-empirical claims (i.e., if chakra 3 makes chakra 4 claims), then those claims need to be tested by rational-empirical means, whereupon they usually fail dramatically (astrology, for example, has consistently failed empirical tests devised by astrologers themselves; see *One Taste*, July 29 and December 21 entries). But astrology is one of the numerous valid worldviews available at the mythic level of consciousness, and it accomplishes what it is supposed to accomplish at that level—provide meaning, a sense of connection to the cosmos, and a role for the self in the vastness of the universe. It is not, however, a rational chakra-4 science with predictive power (which is why it has consistently failed empirical tests). For the same reason, we needn't give much credence to what rational science has to say about chakras 5, 6, or 7.

   When I claim that "all views are correct," I mean it in the general sense of every level having its own important truths that not only disclose that level, but also act as important and necessary ingredients of the higher levels (when differentiated and integrated, or transcended and included). From the mythic level we want to preserve the experience of belonging and the capacity for membership in a community. But within any level of reality, there are more valid and less valid views, as determined *by the criteria of that level*. For example, astrology is part of the mythic level, and there are good and bad astrologers. Although none of them have thus far successfully passed any rational-empirical tests, that is not the actual criteria of the mythic level. The mythic level, like all levels, attempts to provide coherence, meaning, connection to the cosmos, care of others, and pragmatic guidelines. The mythological version of this (of which astrology is a subset) is an interpretive scheme that provides meaning, ethos, mythos, and sanction for the separate self at that level. Mythology and astrology speak to this level in all of us, and, when in touch with that level, provide a wonderful connection to our vital roots. Good astrologers do this in valid and worthy ways, bad astrologers do not (judged within that level). Of course, it is one thing to tap into that lower level, quite another to remain there (or to champion that lower level as if it were the ultimate level of reality). Those making higher claims for astrology, when they cannot be substantiated, are suspect in any case.

On the other hand, a rational scientist who despises every variety of mythology because it is a lower level (and cannot pass rational-empirical tests) is simply someone out of touch with his or her roots. Integrated individuals are comfortable with all of the levels of reality as manifested in and through them, and can speak the languages of all of the chakras (and memes) as various situations warrant. As always, it is only the exclusive attachment to any one chakra that causes most of the problems.

6. See *Sex, Ecology, Spirituality* (CW6) and *Sociocultural Evolution* (CW4) for an extensive discussion of Bellah's important work.

7. The six "nations" or "states" that Gerzon finds in America today are: *Patria*, or the religious state (which is grounded in mythic-membership [blue] and is often order Right); *Corporatia*, or the capitalist state (which is grounded in egoic-instrumental rationality [orange], often economic libertarians and free Right); *Disia*, or the disaffected (which are generally of either preconventional or postconventional waves—purple/red or green— fighting the conventional blue and orange; often order Left); *Media*, or the informational state (generally orange and free Left); *Gaia*, or the New Age (a combination of pre- and postconventional; heavily green, often order Left, combined with purple and red, often with regressive effect); and *Officia*, or the political class (which cuts across levels, but is mostly blue, orange, and green, reflecting the populations they serve).

8. Political orientation is a type that is available at several levels (you can be Left or Right red, Left or Right blue, Left or Right orange, etc.)—although traditionally Left and Right have often drawn larger audiences from particular levels, with Left attracting, e.g., purple and green, and Right attracting blue. These populations can be easily tracked using an all-quadrant, all-level indexing system.

9. Vertical depth is missing not only in most conventional writers, but in many

alternative, transpersonal, and spiritual writers—one of the main reasons being that many of them are attempting to honor, or are unconsciously immersed in, the green meme and hence are reluctant to even use the notion of holarchy. This "flatland" spirituality is unfortunately quite common, and it often acts to freeze people at their present wave.

10. Huntington raises the issue of the evolutionary versus circular models of history. In my opinion, both views are correct. There are evolutionary waves of development, within which there are cycles, seasons, or phases of development. The former refers to transformational development, the latter to translational development. In many cases, the completion of a cycle opens a system (individual or collective) to a transformation, which may be either transcendental and progressive or disintegrative and regressive. See *Integral Psychology* for a discussion of this theme.

11. At one point Huntington belittles the German distinction between civilization and culture. "German thinkers drew a sharp distinction between civilization, which involved mechanics, technology, and material factors, and culture, which involved values, ideals, and the higher intellectual, artistic, moral qualities of a society." But that is a very real distinction—it is, in fact, the Lower-Right (social) and Lower-Left (cultural) quadrants—and Huntington himself uses both of those (it usually doesn't pay to disagree with Germans when it comes to philosophy). Huntington is objecting to the "sharp" separation of cultural and social, which I agree is a mistake; the quadrants are distinct but not separable, and both need to be included.

Civilizations, as Huntington defines them, are broad cultural patterns (and by "cultural" he means "sociocultural"); they are "comprehensive" ("that is, none of their constituent units can be fully understood without reference to the encompassing civilization"); they show development or evolution ("they are dynamic, they evolve, they adapt"—which can also include decay and death, and usually does); they are not political, but deeper than that ("a civilization may contain one or many political units"). I believe all of those are essentially correct, but I might add a few more points. In my view civilizations are amalgams of various lines or streams (such as values, cognitive styles, language, morals, ethics, customs, and traditions) as they move through various levels or waves (e.g., purple, red, blue, orange, green) as manifested in each of the quadrants (individual, behavioral, cultural, and social). Tracking each of those becomes more feasible with a holonic indexing system.

12. For a discussion of subtle reductionism, see note 1 for chap. 5.

13. When I say these analysts, such as Friedman, Gaddis, and Kennedy, are giving a Web-of-Life or "two-quadrants, no levels" interpretation, I mean that they acknowledge the importance of interior quadrants (e.g., culture, worldviews, values), but they do not recognize the many different levels of those interiors, and thus they collapse them to an indistinguishable entity (called "culture" or some such), and almost instantly make those subservient to the Right-Hand quadrants of finance, markets, national security, world banking

practices, technological globalization, or the ecological Web of Life. Their views—and those of the Web-of-Life theorists—are thus "two-quadrants, no levels" (i.e., subtle reductionism, as indicated in the main text). Alternatively, some systems theorists allow hierarchical levels, and even champion them—but they still only acknowledge Right-Hand realities ("two-quadrant, all levels"), and thus are still rooted firmly in flatland and in subtle reductionism. Still, in taking into account five or six streams within the Right-Hand quadrants (such as finance, global markets, environmental factors, technological advances, and military security), and treating them as holistically interwoven (which is true as far as it goes), they are slowly moving toward a more integral view.

The same might be said for the field of future studies, which is dominated by Right-Hand, flatland schemes that attempt to predict possible futures based on various scenarios. Because these various scenarios lack the data of the interior domains—and because the entire spiral of interior domains nonetheless operates in the real world—the futures scenarios are badly skewed by the lack of a more comprehensive set of initial data points covering all four quadrants. This is one of the major reasons that futures scenarios are usually considerably off the mark when it comes to predicting what populations of real humans will do. An "all-quadrants, all-levels, all-lines" model much more closely approximates how real agents behave in the real world.

14. See *One Taste*, December 15 entry, for a discussion of the necessity to balance interior and exterior development.
15. It is conceivable that, as humanity grows toward an integral culture, that at some distant time—many centuries, perhaps—a single World Civilization will have erased the sharp boundaries between the horizontal tectonic plates that Huntington analyzes: a complete blending of cultures, even genetically. But that will not significantly alter the basic developmental levels through which individuals will still progress. Presumably the cultures will have a center of gravity at yellow, turquoise, or higher (and corresponding institutions and governance), but every human being will still be born at beige and begin its growth through the Spiral, and thus populations will still span the spectrum of vertical memes. The human being is a compound individual (a holon), composed of all past subholons (e.g., humans still *contain* atoms, molecules, cells, a reptilian brain stem, a paleomammalian limbic system, etc.), and these subholons are not jettisoned when higher holons emerge. The same is true for the interior quadrants. Even if we are at integral, the archaic, magic, mythic, and rational are still with us.
16. See *The Atman Project*; *Up from Eden*; *Eye to Eye*; *Transformation of Consciousness*; *The Eye of Spirit*; *Sex, Ecology, Spirituality*; and *Integral Psychology*.
17. Does this mean that aboriginal tribes, whose cultural center of gravity was purple-magic, had no genuine transpersonal spirituality? Not at all. The cultural center of gravity is simply an *average*; individuals can be above or below that average in their own case. During the magical-purple epoch (c.

50,000 BCE), there is substantial evidence that the most highly evolved individuals (the shamans) evolved at least into the psychic wave of consciousness, either as a permanent adaptation or, more likely, as extended peak or plateau experiences. Neither of those involved skipping stages, as is carefully explained in *Integral Psychology*.

18. See Huston Smith, *Forgotten Truth* and *The World's Religions*; Wilber, *Integral Psychology*; Roger Walsh, *Essential Spirituality*; Underhill, *Mysticism*; Trungpa, *Shambhala: Sacred Path of the Warrior*; Murphy, *The Future of the Body*.

One of the most common versions of the Great Chain shows up in the East (and often in the West) as the seven chakras, which represent the various levels of being and knowing that are available to humans. The chakras themselves are said to be subtle energy centers in the human organism that support correlative types of knowing and being. They are generally given as seven in number, located at: the base of the body; the genital region; the abdomen; the heart region; the throat; the forehead; the crown. There are also said to be numerous auxiliary chakras above and below those (e.g., the acupuncture meridians are variations on these subtle energy currents).

Of course, there are those who would dismiss the chakras as superstitions, but let us more charitably take a truly multicultural stance and assume that an idea found in virtually every Eastern civilization is something more than mere superstition to be dismissed by superior Westerners, and let us attempt instead to see any wisdom that might be contained therein. For the essential fact is that the seven chakras are simply a slightly more sophisticated version of matter (1), body (2), mind (3-4), soul (5-6), and spirit (7).

For this discussion, I will use the following general correlations (if you have your own favorite version of the chakras, you are welcome to use that, since this example depends only on the notion of seven structural modes of

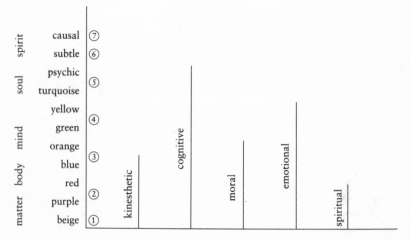

Figure 6-3. Chakras

consciousness, and you can fill in the details however you like). The chakras are very difficult to define, since they serve different functions when they are open or closed. With that caveat, I will loosely define the chakra-levels as: (1) matter (and the archaic worldview, beige); (2) biological life force, prana, emotional-sexual energy, libido, élan vital, magical (purple); (3) lower-mind, including power and conformity, mythic (red/blue); (4) middle-mind, including reason and the beginning of deeper emotions such as love (orange to green); (5) higher-mind, second tier to psychic opening (yellow to coral), creative vision, early stages of spiritual and transcendental consciousness, nature mysticism; (6) subtle consciousness, gnosis, genuine archetypes, deity mysticism; (7) radiant spirit, both manifest and unmanifest, the Abyss, the empty Ground, formless mysticism. These general correlations can be seen in figure 6-3. For the important ways in which the idea of levels of being and knowing—from Spiral Dynamics to the Great Chain to the seven chakras—can be used in cross-level analysis, see note 19.

19. In order to discuss the notion of *cross-level analysis*, and in order to avoid any Eurocentric bias, I will use the chakra system (see note 18). But this analysis is applicable to all developmental schemes, from Spiral Dynamics to Jane Loevinger to Robert Kegan to Jenny Wade to Carol Gilligan. And because these basic waves are virtually universal, they certainly apply to Westerners as well as Easterners.

As we have suggested, the seven chakras, because they represent levels of reality, can be used to classify worldviews according to the chakra from which they originate, and numerous theorists have done exactly that. To give a few examples that various theorists have suggested, we have: materialistic worldviews, such as Hobbes and Marx, stem from chakra 1; vital and pranic worldviews, such as Freud and Bergson, stem from chakra 2; power worldviews, such as Nietzsche, from chakra 3; rational worldviews, such as Descartes, chakra 4; nature mysticism, such as Thoreau, chakra 5; deity mysticism, such as St. Teresa of Avila, chakra 6; and formless mysticism, such as Meister Eckhart, chakra 7.

As useful as those level-of-consciousness classifications are, there are certain problems that immediately stand out, and the only way to handle these difficulties is to introduce what might be called a *cross-level* analysis. For we need to distinguish the level *from which* a worldview originates, and the level *to which* it is aimed. For example, Marx is often taken as an example of a type of materialism (chakra 1), but Marx himself is not coming from chakra 1 or existing at chakra 1. The only thing at chakra 1 is rocks, dirt, inert matter, the physical dimension itself (and the lowest level of consciousness closest to that realm, i.e., archaic-beige). Marx is a very rational thinker; he is coming from, or he is functioning at, chakra 4. But Marx, following Feuerbach, believed that the fundamental realities of the world are essentially material: so he is coming *from* chakra 4, but confining his attention *to* chakra 1. Similarly Freud: his early libido psychology model is coming from chakra 4, but it is aimed at chakra 2. At the other end, so to speak:

the Deists were coming from chakra 4 but aimed at chakra 6 (i.e., a rational attempt to understand Spirit), and so on.

In other words, this allows us to trace both the level of consciousness that the *subject* is coming from, and the level of reality (or *objects*) that the subject believes to be most real. This immediately enriches our capacity to classify worldviews. Moreover, it allows us to do a "double-tracking"—the level of the subject, and the levels of reality the subject acknowledges. This is sometimes referred to as the "levels of selfhood" and the "levels of reality"—or simply the level of the subject and the level of the object. In Huston Smith's maps summarizing the world's great wisdom traditions (figs. 4-1 and 4-2), you can see that he has written "levels of selfhood" and "levels of reality" in each.

Going one step further and showing how these can result in "cross-level" phenomena and "double-tracking" was a procedure introduced in *A Sociable God* and *Eye to Eye* and refined in *Integral Psychology*. For "levels of reality" (or "planes of reality") I also use "realms of reality" (e.g., gross realm, subtle realm, causal realm) or "spheres of reality" (e.g., biosphere, noosphere, theosphere). For "levels of selfhood" I often use "levels of consciousness" or "levels of subjectivity." But I usually refer to them both as basic levels, basic structures, or basic waves, since they are correlative (i.e., there are as many levels of selfhood as there are levels of reality).

The point is that, especially in the middle range (chakras 3, 4, and 5), the subject or self at those chakras can take as an object any of the other chakras (any of the other levels of reality)—can think about them, form theories about them, create artworks of them—and we need to take those into account. Even if we say that only the middle chakras engage in cross-level work (the lower chakras, such as rocks, do not do so; and the higher chakras tend to be transmental, although they can certainly form mental theories—but we will leave them out for simplicity's sake), that means that chakras 3, 4, and 5 can give their attention to each of the seven chakras, forming a different worldview in each case—which gives us *twenty-five major worldviews* available from the seven structural levels of consciousness in the human bodymind. (Seven each from those three, and one each from the other four.) The simple point is that seven levels can support several dozen worldviews!

And, of course, that is just the start. If the holonic conception is "all quadrants, levels, lines, types, states, and realms," we have just briefly discussed *levels of self* (or subject) and levels or *realms* of reality (or objects). For the number of those levels, I generally use anywhere from seven (such as the chakras) to twelve (such as shown in figs. 3-2 and 6-1). The exact number is not as important as the simple recognition of a genuine holarchy of being and knowing.

But we still need to include the *quadrants* in each of those levels; the different *lines* or streams that move through those levels; the various *types* of orientations available at each; and the many altered *states* that temporarily tap into different realms. Moreover, individuals, groups, organizations, nations, civilizations all undergo various kinds of *development* through each of those variables. All of the above factors contribute to different types of worldviews, and all of them need to be taken into account in order to offer a truly integral overview of available worldviews. Still, as I try to demonstrate in the main text, the result is a holistic indexing system that dramatically simplifies the existing jumble. (See note 20.)

20. Of course, in order for these temporary states to become enduring realizations, the person will have to grow and develop through the spiral and into these higher realms as a permanent realization, and not merely as a temporary or nonordinary state: passing *states* must become permanent *traits*. See *Integral Psychology* for an extensive discussion of these topics.

We have seen that there are a few schemes that do attempt to introduce vertical depth by using something like the chakra system itself—e.g., Marx is said to be an example of materialism (chakra 1), Freud is pansexualism (chakra 2), Adler is a type of power psychology (chakra 3), Carl Rogers embraces humanistic psychology (chakra 4), and so on. But most of those schemes, we also saw, fail to take into account cross-level phenomena, and thus the "depth" they offer is badly skewed. Marx, Freud, and Adler are all rational thinkers; they are coming *from* chakra 4 but putting major emphasis on the lower chakras. But the lower chakras *themselves* have worldviews that move from archaic (beige, chakra 1) to *magic* (purple, chakra 2) to mythic (red/blue, chakra 3). At that point, the egoic-rational worldviews emerge (orange/green, chakra 4), and they can take as their *object* any of the other chakras. When chakra 4 believes only chakra 1 is real, we get the rational philosophy of materialism—we get a Hobbes or a Marx. When chakra 4 believes the emotional-sexual dimension is most crucial, we get a Freud. When it puts great emphasis on chakra 3, we get an Adler, and so on.

When chakra 4 looks *above* its own station and *thinks* about higher and transrational domains—*but without actually transforming to those higher domains*—then we get various mental philosophies about spirituality: we get rational Deism (4 aimed at 6), rational systems theory taking Gaia as Spirit (4 aimed at 5), a philosophical concept of the Abyss or Ground of Being (4 aimed at 7), and so on. Those are all still coming from chakra 4, because the subject itself is still at chakra 4 while it thinks about the higher chakras. If the subject (or the level of selfhood) actually transforms to those higher levels of reality, then we have the worldviews *from* those higher chakras. At chakra 5, you do not think about the web of life, you have a direct experience of cosmic consciousness, where you concretely experience being one with the entire gross realm of nature. At chakra 6, you do not think about Platonic archetypes, or merely pray to Deity form, you are rather directly immersed in a living union with Divine Presence. At chakra 7, you are plunged into the formless unmanifest, the Abyss, Emptiness, Urgrund, Ayn, nirvikalpa samadhi, and so on. (See note 19.)

Most religious beliefs are of the purple, red, or blue variety (2nd and 3rd chakras), which constitute around 70 percent of the world's population (which is why the world is indeed "full of religious believers"). But narrow religious belief is one thing; deep spiritual experiences are another. This is why the worldviews *from* those higher levels can only be seen *from* those higher levels. So we make a sharp distinction between being at, say, chakra 3 and having a temporary experience of a higher realm, or simply thinking about higher realms, versus directly being at those higher waves: the actual worldviews are dramatically different in each case.

Index